BULLETIN OF THE JOHN RYLANDS LIBRARY

VOLUME 100 NUMBER 1, SPRING 2024

BULLETIN OF THE JOHN RYLANDS LIBRARY

ISSN 2054-9318 (Print)
ISSN 2054-9326 (Online)

Established in 1903

Members of the Editorial Board 2024

Chair: David Matthews
Editors: Fred Schurink and Rachel Winchcombe
Editorial Assistant: Emma Nelson

Editorial Board

Guyda Armstrong
Paul Fouracre
Roy Gibson
John Hodgson
David Law
Phyllis Mack
Janette Martin
John Morgan
Walter Pohl
Lynda Pratt
Ingrid Rembold
Carsten Timmermann
Huw Twiston Davies

Subscriptions

To subscribe please contact: Manchester University Press Journals Subscriptions, 176 Waterloo Place, University of Manchester, Oxford Road, Manchester, M13 9GP, UK
Tel: +44 (0)161 275 2310
manchesterhive@manchester.ac.uk
https://www.manchesterhive.com/view/journals/bjrl/bjrl-overview.xml

The *Bulletin* is published twice a year. The subscription prices for 2024 are:
Institutions (print and online) £235/$360/€285
Institutions (online only) £200/$295/€235
Individual (print only) £81/$120/€91

The complete archive of the *Bulletin of the John Rylands Library*, from its first issue in 1903 to Volume 80 (1998) is now available to purchase from Manchester University Press. The archive complements the current subscription product (1999 to date), and can be purchased on a one-time basis or as an annual subscription. To obtain pricing information, please contact manchesterhive@manchester.ac.uk.

BULLETIN OF THE JOHN RYLANDS LIBRARY

VOLUME 100 NUMBER 1 SPRING 2024

CONTENTS

Articles

Mills, Manuscripts and Monastic Archives: The Phillipps Charters of Mont Saint-Michel *Richard Allen and Benjamin Pohl*	1
Peter Legh and the Electoral Management of Newton, 1685–1744 *Richard Harrison*	39
Longford Hall Revisited: A New Building Date, and an Architect *Richard Bond*	61
The English Gift after the Destruction of the University of Louvain Library in World War I *Cathleen Hoeniger*	85

Mills, Manuscripts and Monastic Archives: The Phillipps Charters of Mont Saint-Michel

RICHARD ALLEN, UNIVERSITY OF OXFORD
BENJAMIN POHL, UNIVERSITY OF BRISTOL

Abstract

This article examines three medieval charters of the Norman abbey of Mont Saint-Michel, today preserved among the collections of the John Rylands Research Institute and Library. Rare survivors of the destruction of the abbey's archives in 1944, these charters previously formed part of the enormous private library assembled by Sir Thomas Phillipps (1792–1872), antiquarian and bibliophile. They are here studied in detail for the first time, showcasing them not just for what they can tell us about the property to which they relate and the celebrated abbey to which it once belonged, but, more importantly, for what they reveal about the structure and organisation of the lost institutional archive of which they formed a part in the Middle Ages. This article also contextualises these charters within the wider Phillipps collection, exploring questions associated with the antiquarian practice of preserving and presenting medieval documents, a subject which has only recently begun to receive the scholarly attention it deserves.

Keywords: Mont Saint-Michel; Thomas Phillipps; charters; archives; inventory; thirteenth century; fourteenth century

Introduction

This article offers a study, critical edition and translation of three charters of the late twelfth and early thirteenth centuries now housed at Manchester among the collections of the John Rylands Research Institute and Library. Ordinarily, to pay such close attention to these documents might be seen as excessive, given that they are small in number and concern just a single watermill located in the parish of Carolles, in what is today western Normandy.[1] However, neither the monastic institution in whose archives these charters were once found, nor the history of these archives themselves, nor that of the private collection of which they once formed a part, can be considered in any way ordinary. The abbey of Mont Saint-Michel, which was founded, according to legend, in 708 by St Aubert, bishop of Avranches, is one of the most celebrated medieval monasteries north of the Alps.[2] It was not only a major site of pilgrimage, but also a significant landholder in both France and England, as well as an important centre of scholarship and learning. Much of what we know of the medieval abbey's intellectual life has been gleaned from its superb library, the extant volumes of which are today largely housed at the municipal library of Avranches and frequently exhibited in the nearby Scriptorial museum.[3] The abbey's enormous archive, one of the richest of any religious house in medieval France, has not similarly survived. Transferred from Mont Saint-Michel in the wake of the French Revolution to the departmental archives then taking shape at Saint-Lô, the entirety of the abbey's administrative records, including almost all its medieval charters, were destroyed in the Allied bombing of Saint-Lô on 6 June 1944. In the years since, the sheer scale of this loss has been further compounded by the fact that the records of Mont Saint-Michel were still uncatalogued at the time of their destruction, meaning that, while scholars have long had a general idea of how much was lost,[4] it is often difficult to get a precise sense of what exactly perished in the flames of that fateful night.[5]

The three charters now at the John Rylands Library are important survivors of this tragedy. This article examines them in detail for the first time,[6] showcasing them not only for what they can tell us about the property to which they relate and the celebrated abbey to which it once belonged, but also for what they reveal about the structure and organisation of the lost institutional archive of which they formed a part in the Middle Ages. The article is divided into three main parts. The first briefly sets the charters in their current archival milieu by examining how they came to be acquired initially by Sir Thomas Phillipps (1792–1872), antiquary and bibliophile, and then, subsequently, by the John Rylands Library. This helps contextualise the three charters and the album in which they appear within the wider Phillipps collection, which was easily one of the largest private manuscript libraries ever assembled, and addresses important questions of provenance, preservation and presentation. The second part focuses on the monastic archive in which these charters were previously housed by bringing them into conversation with a medieval inventory of Mont Saint-Michel's muniment collection (*chartrier*). It shows how the Rylands charters can help shed light on the creation of this inventory, long known to antiquaries and scholars alike but hitherto little studied, and thus on the organisation of the abbey's later medieval archives. The third and final part then examines the charters themselves and the mill to which they relate, highlighting the wider ways in which a powerful monastic institution like Mont Saint-Michel used such structures to shape and control both the surrounding landscape and its inhabitants. The three charters are edited to critical standards and translated in an appendix, thereby making their texts available both to scholars and students.

Thomas Phillipps, the John Rylands Library and the Charters of Mont Saint-Michel

The three charters that constitute the focus of this article are today part of the Rylands collection known as the Phillipps Charters (PHC). Comprising over 500 acts and other administrative records dating from the twelfth to the seventeenth century, the documents contained therein once formed part of the staggeringly large private library of manuscripts compiled by Sir Thomas Phillipps at Middle Hill, Broadway, in Worcestershire, which was subsequently broken up by sale in the wake of his death in 1872.[7] The Mont Saint-Michel acts are bound in a single, large album, on the leaves of which are fastened forty documents of various kinds and origin but which mainly relate to French ecclesiastical institutions (PHC/28–67). It was one of two such albums acquired by the John Rylands Library during a sale of Phillipps manuscripts held on 6 June 1910 (the other is now PHC/68–125), the Sotheby's catalogue for which describes them as 'Chartæ antiquæ ad monasteria diversa spectantes'.[8] Assigned the Rylands accession number R23196 (1/2), the album was subsequently described to item level by Robert Fawtier in a hand-list published in this journal in 1924, and in book-form the following year.[9]

The story of how the three Mont Saint-Michel charters arrived at the John Rylands Library is, therefore, a relatively straightforward one to relate. The same cannot be said for how Thomas Phillipps first acquired them. The sheer scale of the Phillipps collection – which at some 60,000 individual items was significantly larger than those of most public institutions – and the somewhat unorthodox ways in which it was administered both during and after Phillipps's lifetime, mean that anyone attempting to trace the provenance of a particular manuscript (or, alternatively, its current resting place) must navigate a labyrinthine archival and bibliographical landscape.[10] In fact, one of the only apparent certainties in our case is the Phillipps manuscript number assigned to the album in which the Mont Saint-Michel charters are now bound: 32,288.[11] Such a high number in the Phillipps sequence means it is not among the items catalogued in the 'living text' that is the *Catalogus librorum manuscriptorum in bibliotheca D. Thomæ Phillipps*, which was printed in fascicules by Phillipps himself, ending with item 23,837 at the time of his death.[12] Nor is it among the three inventories made for probate after 1872, one of which goes up to 26,365.[13] Those manuscripts that are described in the printed catalogue had been numbered by Phillipps consecutively in approximate order of acquisition, with the album's number suggesting that it came into his possession towards the end of his life. Such was the scale and mania of his collecting, however, that it is equally possible that the album was acquired at an earlier date and only numbered by Phillipps much later (items purchased on the Continent did not always arrive promptly at Middle Hill);[14] or that its contents were acquired across time in piecemeal fashion and only bound together at a later date; or that it was among those items acquired and numbered earlier, only to be renumbered by Phillipps's grandson, Thomas Fitzroy Fenwick (1856–1938);[15] or that it was among those uncatalogued manuscripts to which numbers were seemingly assigned by those responsible for compiling the above-mentioned probate inventories.[16]

Anyone wanting to try and shed further light on such matters can turn to the Phillipps-Robinson papers, today conserved at the Bodleian Libraries, Oxford, which contain records relating to the Phillipps collection.[17] Rather than offering an ordered list of acquisitions, however, the Phillipps-Robinson papers represent in themselves much of the obsessive – and, at times, quite disordered – mania behind the Phillipps collection, with many volumes being composed of hundreds of scrappy and difficult-to-contextualise notes, written on everything from old envelopes to invitation cards, which have often been brought together in no discernible chronological order. A thorough search of these papers has revealed no apparent explicit mention of either the Mont Saint-Michel charters or the album in which they are now bound. There is also no apparent note from which one might reasonably infer mention of either the charters or the album. That said, the Phillipps-Robinson papers do help illuminate Phillipps's collecting activities, including the provenance of large parts of his library. They also provide important clues as to when, where and on whose initiative the Rylands album acquired its present form. The answers to such questions may not help resolve the central issue of provenance, but they do allow us to contextualise this particular object not just within the Phillipps collection itself, but also within the wider antiquarian practice of preserving and presenting medieval documents in albums and scrapbooks, a subject which has only recently begun to receive the scholarly attention it deserves.[18]

Unsurprisingly, given the size and scope of the Phillipps collection, both the Phillipps-Robinson papers and the incomplete catalogue show that Phillipps regularly acquired individual charters, such as the thirteenth-century act of Andrew, abbot of Santo Stefano del Bosco (*fl.* 1240), listed by Phillipps on 3 June 1869 and described in the final part of the catalogue printed before his death,[19] as well as pre-bound albums of diplomatic material such as the 'Cartæ antiquæ (68) pasted into a vol.', which apparently included documents from the reign of Elizabeth I (1558–1603) to 1789.[20] Determining anything in relation to the Rylands manuscript, therefore, may seem like an impossible task. Fortunately, a previously unknown inventory, which is bound into a volume of miscellaneous lists, *c.*1830–66, helps provide important context. Titled 'Catalogue of ancient charters at Middle Hill, 1848', it is a short list in Phillipps's handwriting of twenty-three eleventh- and twelfth-century charters relating to a range of French ecclesiastical institutions.[21] The items in question are described in sufficient detail so as to allow their current location to be identified, with the majority today being conserved at the Bibliothèque nationale de France (hereafter BnF) in MS nouv. acq. lat. 2588.[22] At the beginning of the twentieth century, the items in this manuscript were still at Thirlestaine House, Cheltenham, to which Phillipps had moved from Middle Hill in the latter part of his life, and were among 272 of his manuscripts acquired by the BnF in 1908.[23] Although the abovementioned list shows that some of the Paris charters were in Phillipps's possession as early as 1848, suggesting that he perhaps acquired them during one of his collecting trips to the Continent in 1822–23 and 1827–29,[24] the reverse of four of them bear the Phillipps manuscript number 24,807.[25] This means that not only are they missing from those manuscripts described in the unfinished printed catalogue, but also that we should not necessarily take the high number of the Rylands albums to suggest that they were acquired by Phillipps towards the end of his life. Some charters in MS nouv. acq. lat. 2588 bear equally high numbers,[26] with at least one being higher than that of the Rylands manuscripts,[27] while those with numbers low enough to be in the unfinished catalogue are not described in the corresponding entry found therein.[28] As for the Paris manuscript's binding, it is unclear whether its contents were brought together by Phillipps himself or by staff at the BnF, although the latter seems more likely, given that many charters have been fixed into the album in such a way as to obscure information written on their reverse, including Phillipps manuscript numbers, which one imagines Phillipps himself would have wanted to leave visible.[29] Whatever the case may be, the numbers that are still legible on the back of the Paris charters act as a useful guide as to how Phillipps administered those charters which he had acquired individually, or in small batches, and thus help tell us something about the Rylands manuscripts. Indeed, had their contents been acquired as individual items, subsequently bound together by Phillipps, then one could reasonably expect to see his manuscript numbers on their reverse. Instead, no such numbering appears on any of the charters pasted into either of the two Rylands albums, suggesting – in the absence of concrete evidence to the contrary – that Phillipps acquired them in their current state.

While the identity of the person who first compiled and assembled the Rylands manuscripts must, for the time being, remain unknown, one thing we can say with certainty is that the documents they contain are presented neither haphazardly nor randomly, much less accidentally, but selectively according to 'themes'.[30] This is true of the internal sequencing of items within each album and their particular arrangement and juxtaposition, with individual pages or page sequences sometimes representing different 'sub-themes' – indeed, the three closely related Mont Saint-Michel charters are themselves a perfect example of this (Figure 1). Similarly, while Phillipps's desire to collect was driven by a seemingly inexhaustible mania, he by no means acquired items like the Rylands albums as mere curiosities or status symbols, but instead as objects whose contents might be shared with other like-minded individuals. As is well documented, these regularly included antiquarians and historians, such as Sir Frederic Madden (1801–73), whose musings on the chaotic state of Middle Hill are well known,[31] and the renowned German medievalist Georg Heinrich Pertz (1795–1876), whom the Phillipps-Robinson papers show consulted almost 270 manuscripts during a visit to Middle Hill in 1845 (the Rylands albums were not among them).[32] Voracious though Phillipps's collecting habits may have been, it was not an obsession he kept to himself, with items like the Rylands albums preserving and presenting their contents in such a way as to become finding aids through which readers like Pertz and others, some of whom continued to be granted access to Phillipps's collection after his death, might engage with material that, prior to their collation and compilation, had been in far less accessible private collections or religious archives.[33] Even if it seems that Phillipps may not necessarily have been responsible for compiling the two Rylands albums himself, it is certainly not unreasonable to say that they are just the sort of objects he would nevertheless have been happy to create and make available for consultation by his peers.

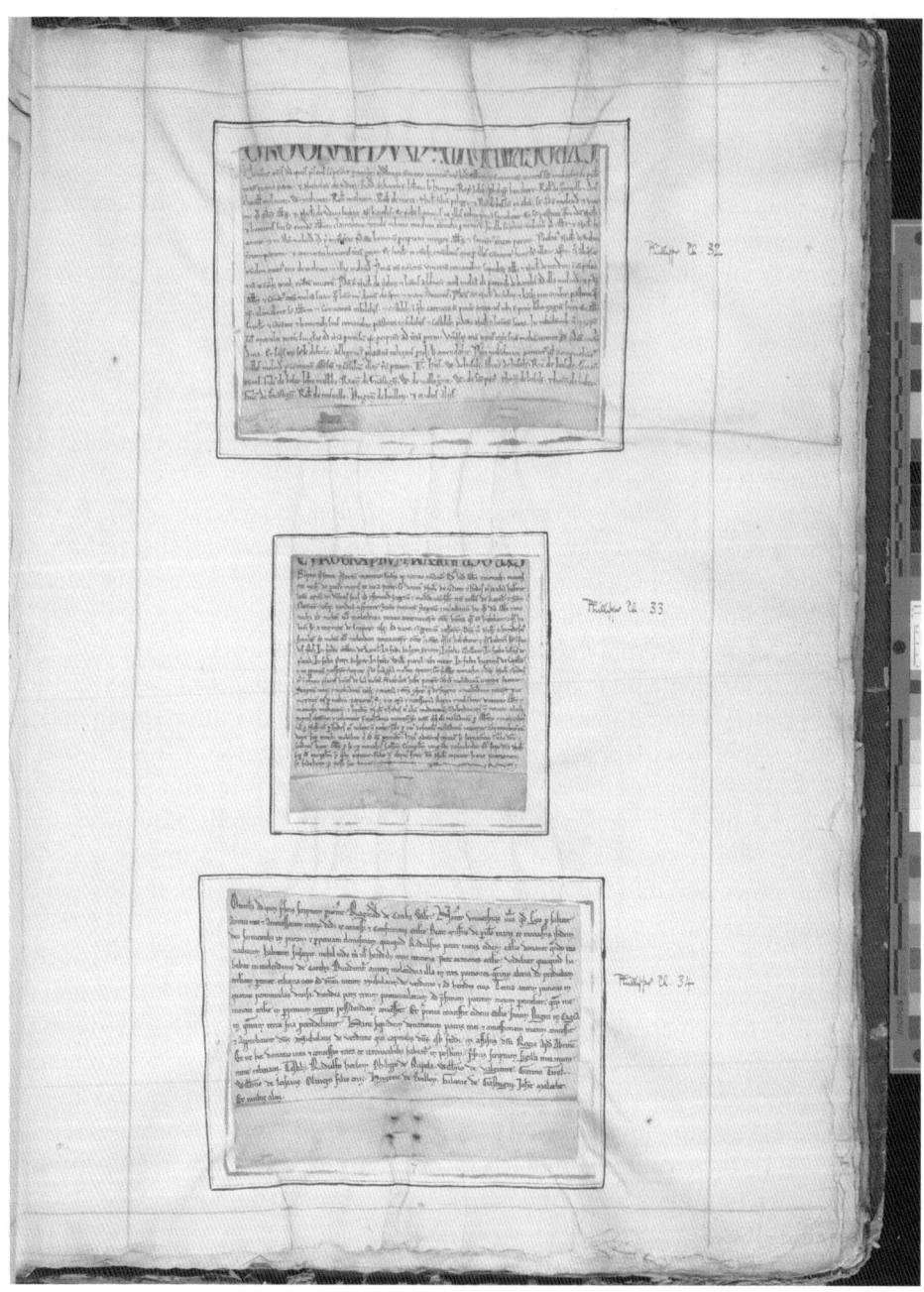

Figure 1 The Mont Saint-Michel charters at the John Rylands Library (PHC/32–34). Copyright © The University of Manchester Library.

The Monastic Archives of Mont Saint-Michel and Their Medieval Organisation

It is important to note that Phillipps began amassing his collection at a propitious time. The 1820s and 1830s saw many private libraries come on the market, with Phillipps able to purchase large collections containing manuscripts of French origin from fellow collectors and bibliophiles, such as Charles Chardin (1742–1826), Luigi Celotti (1759–1843) and Frederick North, later 5th Earl of Guilford (1766–1827), to name but a few.[34] Not all of these collections had been legitimately acquired by their previous owners, however, and Phillipps was among those English antiquarians and bibliophiles able to profit from the still-chaotic post-revolutionary state of the provincial archives in France, where Norman repositories like the nascent Archives départementales du Calvados were at the mercy of men such as the abbé Gervase de la Rue (1751–1835),[35] who had few qualms about 'borrowing' items for his own private library from the collections under his self-appointed protection, some of which eventually made their way into Phillipps's hands.[36] It was via such channels that the compiler of the Rylands volumes most likely acquired their contents, although the precise point at which the three Mont Saint-Michel charters in 32,288 (PHC/28–67) were extracted from the abbey's archives can only be reasonably guessed at. While still housed at Mont Saint-Michel, the abbey's muniment collection seems to have suffered relatively few losses to borrowing or theft, although there is evidence of at least one charter being removed before the French Revolution, or so it would seem.[37] What is more, unlike the Archives du Calvados, those for the neighbouring department of La Manche, housed first at Coutances and then, from 1800, at Saint-Lô, were administered during their early years by the reputable figures of Jérôme-Jean Costin (1759–1825) and François-Nicolas Dubosc (1815–86), neither of whom are known to have engaged in the sort of malfeasance practised by de la Rue. That said, the experiences of collectors like Jeremiah Holmes Wiffen (1792–1836) show that English antiquarians could still have unfettered access to the rich collections at Saint-Lô even as late as the second half of the 1820s, allowing them to purloin items (including charters of Mont Saint-Michel) as a result.[38]

With this in mind, let us now turn to look at an important but little studied fourteenth-century inventory of the abbey's archive, and at the ways in which the Rylands charters, which are listed therein, help shed new light on its creation. Before turning to the inventory in earnest, however, a brief recapitulation of the history of the Mont Saint-Michel archives between the eleventh and fourteenth centuries is required. For the earlier part of this period, nothing is known about either the organisation of the abbey's archival records or the location in which they were kept. No extant document from the eleventh and twelfth centuries refers explicitly to Mont Saint-Michel's collection of charters (*chartrier*), while no part of the Romanesque monastic complex has ever been definitively identified as the space in which this collection was housed. That said, the abbey's famous cartulary, begun most likely under Abbot Bernard (1131–49) or Abbot Geoffrey (1149–50/51), provides evidence of the monastic community's care and maintenance of its archive in the first half of the twelfth century,[39] while it has recently been argued that Geoffrey's celebrated successor, Robert of Torigni (1154–86), may have kept his community's charter collection, which was then most probably a portable affair stored in a single chest, in his abbatial chambers.[40] It is not until the later Middle Ages, however, that we have explicit evidence relating to the ways in which the abbey's archives were organised and conserved. The most obvious is the abbey's two-storey muniment tower (*tour du chartrier*), which is attached to the north-western corner of the structure today known as '*la Merveille*' (Figure 2). According to the monk-historian

Figure 2 The muniment tower (*tour du chartrier*) of Mont Saint-Michel. Copyright © Richard Allen.

Thomas Le Roy (1618–83), this tower was built in 1406 by Abbot Pierre Le Roy (1384–1411) as part of a systematic reorganisation of the abbey's archives, although architectural historians have long noted the presence of certain thirteenth-century features in the tower's lower chamber that suggest a much earlier date of construction.[41]

The other major extant record of activity with regard to the archives is the fourteenth-century inventory itself, which refers to the small cupboards or chests (*armariola*) in which the charters were then kept.[42] It is difficult to know precisely what prompted the inventory's creation at this point in time, but it is worth mentioning that the early fourteenth century was a period in which troubles between England and France had a material impact on the abbey's possessions, which might well have prompted a 'stocktaking' of its existing rights and privileges.[43] It is also possible that the inventory was drawn up in the context of moving the archives permanently into the muniment tower, and/or reorganising them in preparation for the creation of a register or cartulary. This was certainly the case during the abbacy of Pierre Le Roy, who, according to a short in-house *gesta*, went through the archives himself in preparation for making various inventories and registers, including a now lost cartulary, known as the *Livre blanc*, and a lost rental, known as the *Quanandrier*.[44] As we shall see in the conclusion, it is possible that a second inventory, itself also lost, was produced at around the same time.

The surviving inventory considered here is today housed at the municipal library at Avranches in MS 211, a composite volume, the first part of which is formed of historiographical texts.[45] If one is to believe a note found at the bottom of its final folio, the inventory was written in 1326,[46] although there are at least two acts listed with dates after this *terminus ad quem*.[47] Largely the work of a single scribe, the inventory lists 1,490 acts in total and is divided into twenty-seven sections, four of which are general (e.g., *Emptiones*) and the rest geographical, relating to places where the abbey had a priory.[48] Three of the four general sections specifically identify the name of the cupboard/chest (*armariolum*) in which the corresponding acts were kept (the '*armariolum Montis*' for royal/ducal acts and purchases, and the '*armariolum privilegiorum*' for papal bulls), while a note at the inventory's beginning, and another found next to a charter listed under the heading for '*Sanctus Paternus*' (that is, Saint-Pair-sur-Mer),[49] suggest that the inventory reflects not an original ordering made in the process of its creation but rather an existing system of organisation similar to that still found in the muniment tower of Magdalen College, Oxford, where deeds from the early twelfth century to the early sixteenth are kept in fifteenth-century wooden boxes labelled by place (Figure 3).[50]

Whatever the case may be, ordering items geographically was not without its complications, since even a quick glance reveals that certain acts have been listed twice because their content related to benefices situated in different places. Moreover, the same act is sometimes listed twice under the same heading since the abbey's archives were home to two copies of it. Alongside the uncertainties caused by duplicate entries, it is also worth noting that only 399 acts are listed with a specific date (27 per cent of the total), of which 307 (that is, 77 per cent of the dated total) are for the period after 1250. It is therefore difficult to know precisely which period many

Figure 3 Fifteenth-century deed boxes in the muniment tower of Magdalen College, Oxford. Copyright © Richard Allen.

acts belong to, as the descriptions can sometimes be both vague and laconic (e.g., *Littera confirmationis donationum* d'Aufains). It is finally worth remarking that the inventory seems to have been designed to be something of a 'living text'. Significant gaps are left between the final act listed in a section and the next section's heading, suggesting that the inventorist envisaged further entries being made (fol. 123r is left entirely blank, since the final entry in the section for Saint-Pair, where Mont Saint-Michel had many possessions, appears towards the bottom of fol. 122v). In some instances, later scribes did indeed return to add new entries (e.g., fol. 116v), while others added dates and numbers (some Arabic, some Roman) next to certain entries.

One issue that has never been properly explored, however, is the way in which the charters are described. Various terms are employed, both general (*cyrographum, carta, littera, copia*) and specific (*donatio, compositio, financia*), with no obvious rationale behind their usage. That said, in her edition of the abbey's celebrated twelfth-century cartulary, Katharine Keats-Rohan notes how the word '*cyrographum*' seems to have been used by the inventorist not to reflect an act's actual diplomatic form but rather to describe 'charters which bestowed churches that then or later became a priory [. . .] or other important early endowments'.[51] The use of this term is by no means consistent, however, with one twice-inventoried act being styled first as 'cyrographum' and then as 'littera'.[52] As for later acts, these are sometimes described extremely tersely (see the example cited in the previous paragraph for Auffains, which is actually an 1192 charter of Reginald, bishop of Chartres), and other times in much greater detail.[53] It is this element that the Rylands charters help illuminate, via nothing more complicated than the endorsements found on their reverse, which, in two instances, echo exactly the corresponding entry found in the fourteenth-century inventory. As Table 1 illustrates, they are by no means unique in this respect. Nevertheless, this simple yet previously unnoticed connection allows us to examine the reverse of other extant originals afresh and similarly compare them with the corresponding descriptions in the inventory of 1326.

With regard to the Rylands charters themselves, two out of the three (PHC/33 and PHC/34) have a single description of the act's contents on their reverse, which, in both cases, is written in a thirteenth-century hand in dark brown ink. The same hand – or a very similar one – can also be seen penning the descriptions on the reverse of nos 5, 9–10, 13, 15, 18, 20–4 (Figure 4). A second scribe, writing in a much lighter ink, then returned to add above each of these descriptions a Roman numeral that mirrors the numeral assigned to the corresponding entry in the inventory. The third Rylands charter (PHC/32) also has a brief description written in the same hand and ink colour as the other two, above which a second scribe has similarly added a Roman numeral (corresponding, once again, with that found next to the inventory entry) and also a brief – but now almost illegible – addendum to the main description. The most likely reason why the endorsement on this third act does not appear verbatim in the inventory is that its entry follows on directly from that of a now lost charter relating to the same issue, prompting the inventorist to describe its contents in a curtailed form.[54]

A survey of surviving originals conserved elsewhere shows that the inventorist also copied other charter endorsements, the tenor of which is sometimes the result of multiple scribes working across the centuries. Thus, an eleventh-century original at the Archives de la Manche, which is one of a handful of charters that survived the destruction of 1944 because they were then on loan to another repository,[55] and another of the twelfth century, which is among a collection of Mont Saint-Michel acts acquired by the BnF in the early nineteenth century from sources unclear,[56] both have terse twelfth-century endorsements to which the same fourteenth-century scribe has added further precisions, the combination of which has been copied verbatim by the inventorist (nos 4, 13). The same fourteenth-century scribe also made additions to the earlier endorsements found on at least six other originals (nos 5, 16, 18, 20, 23–4). In other instances, however, when the inventorist found nothing on the reverse of a charter but a brief description from an earlier century, he was happy simply to copy this into his inventory (e.g., nos 17, 19). What is more, a number of modern copies, along with a charter now in Paris (no. 25), suggest that the inventorist occasionally came across nothing at all on a charter's reverse, thereby requiring him to describe things in his own terms.[57] It is therefore this apparent adherence to the endorsements that explains the discrepancy between the length of each entry in the inventory and the range of terms it uses.

TABLE 1
Mont Saint-Michel charters: endorsements and inventory entries

	Original charter	Endorsement(s)	Inventory [with folio]
1	Manchester, Rylands, PHC/32	[Litt]era concordiæ inter abbatem Mont(is) et Nich(olaum) de *Verdun* et participes (s.xiii); .VII. (s.xiv); [. . .]p[. . .] [m]olend[ini] de *C(r)apot* (s.xiv).	VII. Item littera concordie de eodem.[83] [fol. 128v]
2	Manchester, Rylands, PHC/33	Littera stagni et molend(ini) de *Carol(es)* (s.xiii); .LVI. (s.xiv).	LVI. Littera stagni et molendini de *Karoles*. Non quotatur.[84] [fol. 127v]
3	Manchester, Rylands, PHC/34	[Ca]rta Rag(inaldi) de Carolis de confirmatione donationis patris sui (s.xiii); .XIII. (s.xiv).	XIII. Carta Rag(inaldi) de *Caroles* de confirmatione donationis patris sui. Non quotatur. [fol. 128v]
4	BnF, MS lat. 9215,[85] no. 59	Carta de *Escai* (s.xii) pro decima quod duo milites nobis ipsum donaverunt inspiciente tota parrochia quam injuste diu tenuerant (s.xiv); .x. (s.xiv).	Carta de *Escay* pro decima quod duo milites nobis ipsum donaverunt inspiciente tota parrochia quam injuste diu tenuerant. [fol. 134r]
5	BnF, MS lat. 9215, no. 62	Recognitio Thome de piscibus ad lardum (s.xiii), videlicet balena, porpes, graspes, [luttes, espaart] (s.xiv).[86]	XI. Recognitio Th(om)e de piscibus ad lardum, videlicet balena, porpeis, graspess, lut(tes), espaart. [fol. 120r]
6	BnF, MS lat. 9215, no. 65	Littera Ph(ilippi) et Petronill(e) ejus uxoris facta Col(ino) de II sol(idos) r(edditus) cum Guillelmo *Beleng(er)* (s.xiv); .109. (s.xv).	109. Item alia littera de venditionis dicti Ph(ilippi) et ejus uxoris videlicet II s(olidos) redditus facta dicto Col(ino) cum Guill(elmo) *Beleng(er)*. M°CCC°XIII°. [fol. 116r]
7	BnF, MS lat. 9215, no. 69	Venditionio Rog(er)i *Le Lonc* de .II. qu(ar)t(eria) fr(ument)i r(edditus) sit(a) in parrochia Sancti Albini (s.xiv); .XCI. (s.xiv); .XXX. (s.xiv).	XCI. Littera venditionis Rog(er)i *Le Lonc*, videlicet II quarteria frumenti in parrochia Sancti Albini sita prout in littera continetur. MCCCXVIII. [fol. 132r]
8	BnF, MS lat. 9215, no. 70	LVII. Compositio inter nos et heredes Pet(ri) *Le Ge(n)till* de Sancto Pat(erno) super hiis que dictus Petrus nobis dederat (s.xiv).	LVII. Compositio inter nos et heredes Pet(ri) *Le Ge(n)til* de Sancto Pat(erno) super hiis que dictus Petrus nobis dederat. MCCCXVIII. Suta cum XIII. [fol. 131v]

	Original charter	Endorsement(s)	Inventory [with folio]
9	BnF, MS lat. 9215, no. 77	Littera Rog(er)i *Murdac* de quatuor sol(idos) qui nobis debentur pro molta masure *Angot* (s.xiii); .XLV. (s.xiv); Carta Rog(er)i *Murdac* de mouta massure *Angot* (s.xiii) pro que debent[ur] nobis IIII^{or} solidorum (s.xiv); .xiii.^{xx} et xv (s. xiv).	XLV. Littera Rog(er)i *Murdac* de quatuor solid(os) qui nobis debentur pro mouta masure *Angot*. [fol. 120v]
10	BnF, MS lat. 9215, no. 79	Littera regis pro Nich(olao) preposito de Donno Joh(ann)e (s.xiii) de compositione inter nos et ipsum super hiis que debet habere (s.xiv); Littera regis pro Nich(olao) preposito de Domno Joh(ann)e (s.xiii).	Littera regis pro Nich(ola)o preposito de Domno Joh(ann)e de compositione inter nos et ipsum super hiis que debet habere. [fol. 135r]
11	BnF, MS lat. 9215, no. 84	Financia quod non cogamur vendere nec extra al(iud) ponere manerium de Cureceyo et de Acigneyo et cetera que hic co(n)tine(n)t(ur) (s.xiv).	Financia quam non cogamur vendere nec extra aliud ponere manerium de Cureio et de Acigneio et cetera que hic continentur. M^{o}CC^o nonagesimo VI. [fol. 115v]
12	BnF, MS lat. 9215, no. 89	CCIII. Littera ven(ditionis) Guill(elmi) Jord(ani) de grangia de Sancto Albino (s.xiv); Littera vend(itionis) Guill(elm)i *Jourdan* de grangia de Sancto Albino (s.xv).	CCIII. Item littera grangie de Sancto Albino empta a Guill(elm)o *Jord(an)*. [fol. 122v]
13	Arch. dép. Manche, 1 H 1	Carta de Perrella (s.xii) quam dedit nobis G. *Pichenout* cum assensu Guill(elm)i comitis Normann(ie) (s.xiv); De Perrevilla (s.xii); De P(er)rella in Guernerreyo (s.xiii).	Carta de Perrella quam dedit nobis G. *Pichenout* cum assensu Guill(elm)i comitis Norma(n)n(ie). [fol. 136r]
14	Arch. dép. Manche, 1 H 2	De Silleio (s.xii); Littera vinearum de Silleio (s.xiv).	Littera vinearum de Sylleyo. [fol. 119r]
15	Arch. dép. Manche, 1 H 3	Carta Gaufredi comitis Andeg(avensis) (s.xii) de celario Sancti Victur(ii) (s.xiii).	Carta Gaufredi comitis Andeg(avensis) de celario Sancti Victurii. [fol. 119r]

(*table continues*)

	Original charter	Endorsement(s)	Inventory [with folio]
16	Arch. dép. Manche, 1 H 4	Insula de Guernercio (s.xii); Carta Pet(r)i filii Desid(er)ie (s.xii) qui sese obtulit cum tota heredit(ate) sua et factus fuit monachus cum concessu ux(oris) sue (s.xiv).	Carta Pet(r)i filii Desiderie qui sese obtulit cum tota hereditate sua et factus fuit monachus cum concessu uxoris sue. [fol. 136r]
17	Arch. dép. Manche, 1 H 5	Carta Symonis de Ballolio (s.xii); Carta Symonis de Ballolio (s.xiii).	Carta Symonis de Baillolio. [fol. 119r]
18	Arch. dép. Manche, 1 H 6	Carta Algari episcopi de eclesia sancti Germani de Carteraio (s.xii); Littera Reymardi de Quartereio de decima ejusdem ville (s.xiii) et dono ecclesie et confirmatio Ph(ilipp)i filii sui qui nobis dedit cum predictis decimam molend(inorum) suorum et duas plateas terre in G(er)seyo (s.xiv).	Littera Raymardi de Qu(ar)tereio de decima ejusdem ville et dono ecclesie et confirmatio Philippi filii sui qui nobis dedit cum predictis decimam molendinorum suorum et duas plateas terre in Gerseio. [fol. 135v]
19	Arch. dép. Manche, 1 H 11	Carta Ric(ardi) filii Ricoloni de Bouceio (s.xii); Pro decima de *Boucey* (s.xv) et pro IIII^{or} acris terre (s.xv).	Carta Richardi filii Ricoloni de *Boucey*. [fol. 116v]
20	Arch. dép. Manche, 1 H 12	Carta decime de P(er)rela in Guernerreyo (s.xiii); Littera quod W(i)ll(elmu)s sacerdos de *Ivetot* cum fratre suo et filio quitaverunt nobis quicquid clamabant super decimam de P(er)rela et omnes pertin(entes) ejus in terra et melagio (s.xiv).	Littera quod Will(elm)us sacerdos de *Yvetot* cum fratre suo et filio quitaverunt nobis quidquid clamabant super decimam de P(er)rela et omnes pertin(entes) ejus in terra et melagio. [fol. 136r]
21	Arch. dép. Manche, 1 H 13	Carta ecclesie de Ponte Ursonis (s.xiii).	Item confirmatio easdem a Rothomag(ensi) archiepiscopo. [fol. 116v]
22	BL, Add. Ch. 66980	De Thoma de Sancto Joh(ann)e (s.xii); Cirographum Th(om)e de Sancto Joh(anne) (s.xiii); .IX. (s.xiv)	IX. Carta de reconciliatione inter nos et Th(om)am de Sancto Joh(ann)e de Th(om)as. MCXXI. IX. Item alia sub eodem tenore. MCXXI. [fol. 128v]

	Original charter	Endorsement(s)	Inventory [with folio]
23	BL, Add. Ch. 15284	Littera messerie de *Genez* quam Garn(er)ius *Rossel* et uxor ejus vendiderunt nobis (s.xiv);.XCII. (s.xiv); III^{CC}XLIII (s.xiv/s.xv).	XCII. Littera messerie de *Genez* quam Garneri(us) *Roussel* et uxor ejus vendiderunt nobis. MCCXXXVII. [fol. 128r]
24	BL, Add. Ch. 15287	Littera Rob(er)to [*sic*] Patricii de terra de Rosello de Grener' (s.xiii) quam [dedit] nobis (s.xiv).	Carta Roberti Patricii et ejus uxoris quod dederunt nobis in Guernerreio terram que fuit Hugoni de Rosello. Item alia de eodem. [fol. 135v]
25	BnF, MS lat. 5430A, p. 294	Compositionem inter episcopum et capitulum Abr(incense), ex una parte, et abbatem et conventum Mo(n)tis, ex altera, super juribus in villa Montis et intra secta monasterii (s.xv).	29. Item littere agentes inter episcopum et capit(ulum) Ab(r)inc(ensis) et nos, videlicet due compositiones unius tenoris, unius episcopus et unius dati et die. M°CC°XXXVI. [fol. 114r]

	Modern Copy	Endorsement(s) [according to copyists]	Inventory [with folio]
26	Allen, 'Unknown copies', Appendix II, no. 5	Littera Rad[ulfi] de Argogiis presbiteri de manerio de *Cruce* (s.xiii) et pluribus aliis (s.xiv).	Littera Rad(u)lphi de Argogiis presbiteri de manerio de *Cruce* et pluribus aliis. [fol. 116v]
27	Arch. dép. Calvados, 1 J 3	Compromissum inter episcopum, capitulum et nos (n.d.).	37. Item compromissio inter episcopum Ab(r)inc(ensem), capitulum et nos. M°CC°XXXII°. [fol. 114r]
28	Arch. dép. Calvados, 1 J 3	Littera quod abbas non potest cogi ut sine monachi residentes apud *Ardevon* nec apud Sanctum Clementem (n.d.).*[87]	38. Item quod abbas non potest cogi ut sine monachi residentes apud *Ardevo(n)* nec apud Sanctum Cleme(n)te(m) et de portione altalagii Po(n)tis Ursonis. M°CC^{mo}XXXII°. [fol. 114r]
29	Arch. dép. Calvados, 1 J 4	Littera Hamonis de Bello Visu de redditibus de Bello Visu et de Passibus (s.xii).	11. Item littera Hamonis de B(e)llo Visu super donatione redditus de B(e)llo Visu et de Passibus. [fol. 115r]
30	Arch. dép. Calvados, 1 J 4	Littera Guillelmi de Valle *Grente* pro viridaria (n.d.).	16. Littera Guill(elm)i de B(e)llo Visu de Viridaria et aliis. [fol. 115r]

(*table continues*)

TABLE 1 (*continued*)

	Modern Copy	Endorsement(s) [according to copyists]	Inventory [with folio]
31	Arch. dép. Calvados, 1 J 4	Littera domini de Bello Visu (n.d.).	35. Littera domini de Bello Visu. [fol. 115r]
32	Arch. dép. Calvados, 1 J 4	Donatio Petri de Sancto Hylario de ecclesia de *Boce* (n.d.).*	Donatio Pet(r)i de Sancto Hyllario de ecclesia de *Bouce*. [fol. 116v]
33	Arch. dép. Calvados, 1 J 4	Littera regis de ecclesia de Ponte Ursonis (n.d.).*	Littera regis Anglie de ecclesia de Po(n)te Urs(onis). [fol. 116v]
34	Arch. dép. Calvados, 1 J 4	Carta Roberti de Grandivilla pro patronatu de *Breville* (n.d.).	XVII. Carta Rob(er)ti de Gr(a)ndivilla pro patronatu de *Breville* super duobus quarteriis frumenti per manum Nicholai de *Maleis*. [fol. 120r]
35	Arch. dép. Calvados, 1 J 4	Carta Nielli de Sancta Columba cum consuetudinibus a G. Normannorum duce confirmata (n.d.).*	Carta Nielli de Sancta Colu(m)ba cum consuetudinibus a G. Norman(n)or(um) duce confirmata. [fol. 123v]
36	Arch. dép. Calvados, 1 J 4	Carta Guillelmi prepositi de *Fouquereville* (n.d.).*	Carta Guill(elm)i prepositi de *Fouquereville*. [fol. 123v]
37	Arch. dép. Calvados, 1 J 4	Littera captionis aguillarum de Molendino Comitis (n.d.).*	L. Littera captionis aguillarum de Molendino Comitis et de Alneto pro reparatione predicti molendini. MCXCVIII. [fol. 127v]
38	Arch. dép. Calvados, 1 J 4	Littera Petri comitis B(r)itannie de custodia terrarum nostrarum Britannie (n.d.).*	7. Littera Pet(r)i comitis de *Richemo(n)t* et ducis B(r)ita(n)nie de custodia terrarum nostrarum de B(ri)ta(n)nia. [fol. 133r]
39	Arch. dép. Calvados, 1 J 4	Littera Symonis *Crasseteste* et Jacobi fratris ejus (n.d.).*	Littera Symonis *Grasseteste* et Jacobi fratris ejus super inundationem aque que cadit a vivario Do(m)ni Joh(ann)is. [fol. 134v]
40	Arch. dép. Calvados, 1 J 4	Carta Henrici de Altaribus de vivario Donni Johannis (n.d.).*	Carta He(n)rici de Altaribus de vivario Do(m)ni Joh(ann)is quod si aliquo dampnum eveneret ei super inundatione aque magistri vivarii condonat nobis et quod tenetur nobis aque ductum de nostro vivario cadentis per terram suam garantizare. [fol. 135r]

	Modern Copy	Endorsement(s) [according to copyists]	Inventory [with folio]
41	Arch. dép. Calvados, 1 J 4	Carta Balduini filii *Homenes* (n.d.).*	Carta Balduini filii *Homenes* qui nobis reddidit terram sitam inter culturam sancti Mich(ael)is et *Torpol* quamdiu injuste *Homenes*. [fol. 135v]
42	Arch. dép. Calvados, 1 J 4	Littera Philippi de *Carteret* pro prioratu de *la Vic* (n.d.).*	Littera Ph(ilipp)i de Carthereto pro prioratu de *Layc* quod dedit nobis XXIX pertic(atas) terre que modo sita est juxta magnum clausum monachorum. [fol. 135v]
43	Arch. dép. Manche, 6 J 70, M2	Littera donationis Sancti Broeladrii (n.d.).	Littera donationis Sancti Broel-(adrii) super pluribus terris et decimis ac partibus ecclesiarum et continet in se duo dona sub duobus nominibus. [fol. 124r]

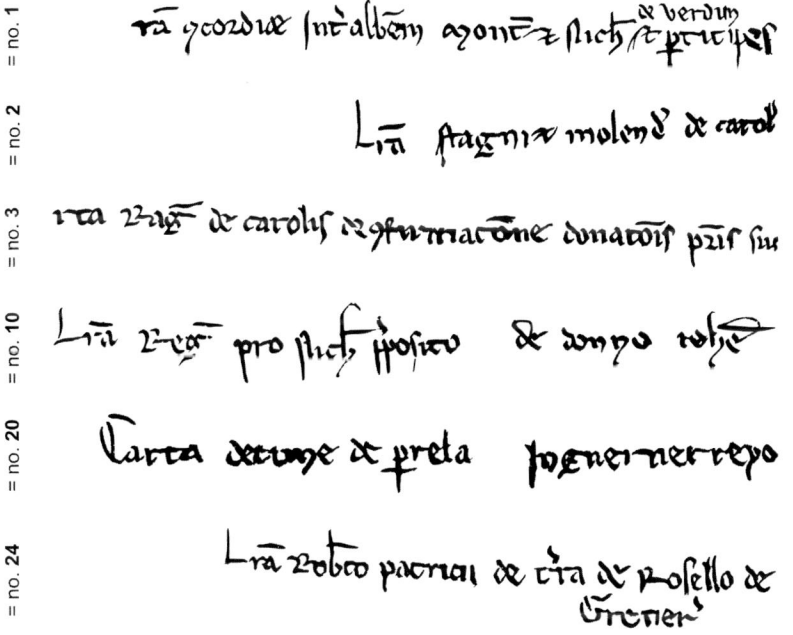

Figure 4 Thirteenth-century endorsements from extant Mont Saint-Michel originals. Copyright © Benjamin Pohl.

Unfortunately, none of the charters it describes as '*cyrographum*' is known to survive as an original, such that we cannot say for certain whether these descriptions were inspired by their endorsements. That said, two originals do contain later endorsements describing each act as a '*cirographum*', one of which (no. 22) is written in the same thirteenth-century hand found on the reverse of the Rylands charters.[58] It is possible, therefore, that similar endorsements were found on the originals since lost or destroyed and described in the inventory using these terms.

The endorsements on the surviving originals found at the John Rylands Library and elsewhere also allow us to say something about the numbering systems used in certain parts of the inventory. Eight of the twenty-seven sections have numbers written next to their entries.[59] Like the dates that also appear there, it is clear that some of these numbers have been added to the inventory after the fact by scribes other than the main inventorist. In the case of the royal/ducal acts and purchases listed in the '*armariolum Montis*', therefore, the position on the page of the inventory's various textual elements allows us to say that the main entries were, by and large, written first (some were added by later scribes), after which a second scribe added dates in Roman numerals, squeezing these in wherever possible. A third scribe, working in the fifteenth century, then returned to write Arabic numerals next to almost every entry. These are again squeezed in wherever possible, including around the already-present dates. The same pattern of composition is evident in the subsequent section for the acts relating to Ardevon.[60] In this instance, one of the charters inventoried under this heading still survives as an original, on the reverse of which is written the same Arabic numeral as appears next to it in the inventory (no. 6). Given the date at which these numerals must have been added, both to the inventory and to the reverse of this particular charter, it is possible that what we have here is a remnant of the work of Abbot Pierre Le Roy, who, as noted, went through the abbey's archives himself in preparing the lost cartulary known as the *Livre blanc*. As for the entries numbered using Roman numerals, these numbers appear to have been added before the dates found in these sections, since they almost always appear in the generous left-hand margin in front of the description, while the dates (also in Roman numerals) appear either at the end of a description or are inserted interlineally. By contrast, in the sections with Arabic numerals, the dates are at times written in the left-hand margin, something which happens almost consistently in one section without any numbering whatsoever.[61]

It is difficult to say whether all these numbers were added at the same time as the descriptions, but the sections in which the Rylands charters are listed, where the numbering and descriptions could easily be by the same scribe (and definitely show no major difference in ink colour, which is not the case elsewhere), suggest this is likely. If so, then this would imply that the inventorist simply copied a numbering system that could already be found on the reverse of these charters, with this system standing as evidence of a previously unknown attempt to arrange a part of the abbey's archive. If not, then it is possible that the inventory was used to help establish this arrangement. Interestingly, seven of the eight sections with a numbering system list the abbey's most prestigious charters or its largest collections thereof, suggesting that priority had been given to their systemisation.[62]

Mills, Monks and Landscape in the Bay of Mont Saint-Michel

Let us lastly turn to examine the contents of the three Rylands charters. Although Robert Fawtier's brief description of them has been in print for a century, the acts have garnered little scholarly attention beyond occasional cursory references.[63] At first glance, this may seem entirely appropriate, given that, as noted at the outset, they concern but a single watermill in western Normandy, located in the parish of Carolles, just fifteen kilometres (as the crow flies) from Mont Saint-Michel. Such apparent disinterest, however, stands in stark contrast to scholarly examination of Mont Saint-Michel's charters in general, which has long been informed by the abbey's celebrated cartulary and the well-known copies of its acts made by Roger de Gaignières (1642–1715), Amédée-Louis Léchaudé d'Anisy (1772–1857) and Léopold Delisle (1826–1910).[64] These modern copies are today of much greater value than when first created, but they by no means capture the totality of the abbey's charter collection at that time (the same can also be said of the cartulary in relation to Mont Saint-Michel's twelfth-century archive). For the period before 1250, copyists like de Gaignières also gave priority less to what we might call 'everyday' acts, into which category the charters at the John Rylands Library can be placed, and more to those issued by popes, kings, dukes, leading aristocrats, bishops and well-respected abbots (especially the almost omnipresent Robert of Torigni). Heretofore unnoticed by both medieval and modern copyists, the Rylands charters therefore offer further important perspective on the ways in which Mont Saint-Michel both managed its vast estates and shaped the landscape of the frontier diocese in which it was located, much like the copies of the abbey's acts recently rediscovered among the Henry Chanteux (1904–95) collection at the Archives du Calvados.[65]

The Rylands charters are also worthy of detailed study because two of them date from the reign of Abbot Jordan (1191–1212), a somewhat enigmatic but nevertheless important figure in Mont Saint-Michel's history. Formerly a monk of the abbey, Jordan was the first person to occupy the abbacy for any considerable length of time after his illustrious predecessor, Robert of Torigni, in whose imposing memory and shadow he perhaps then lived and certainly lives today.[66] In fact, Jordan's abbacy is commonly remembered for two things: the destruction of the abbey by fire in 1204 at the hands of Breton troops, and the serious accusations brought against him before the pope by his monks a few years later. Given such circumstances, scholars have long painted Jordan in a less than favourable light.[67] But, if the final years of his abbacy were no doubt troubled, the diplomatic sources nevertheless show Jordan to have been an active administrator not too dissimilar to Robert of Torigni. His extant – and heretofore little studied – acts relate to a range of Mont Saint-Michel's possessions, though it is the abbey's mills that figure most regularly and prominently, especially during the first decade of his abbacy. Two acts of 1194 and 1196 therefore concern the agreements reached under Jordan with regard to the mill of Mont Rouault, in Brittany, and those of Saint-Jean, located just outside Le Mans on the River Sarthe.[68] Another, of 1202, relates to the mill at Bacilly, known as Moulin-le-Comte, in the bay of Mont Saint-Michel.[69] It is to this same period that

Jordan's two acts for the mill at Carolles (PHC/32 and 33) likely date, as both make mention of the local lord, Nicholas de Verdun (1199–1231), head of an Anglo-Norman family whose estates in Normandy were lost to Philip Augustus in 1204.[70]

Mills were an important source of revenue for any monastic institution, even if not every abbey or priory necessarily chose to exploit them in exactly the same way.[71] The region in and around the parish of Carolles was one given over heavily to cereal cultivation, while its concentrated network of river valleys lent itself particularly well to the installation of watermills, such that Mont Saint-Michel was not the only monastery to have mills there in the twelfth century.[72] To some extent, therefore, it is hardly surprising to find frequent mentions of such structures among the abbey's charters. That said, the medieval mill was, to borrow the expression of Daniel Pichot, an 'instrument of domination' (*instrument de domination*) in the locality,[73] one that played a key role in what Robert Fossier called the '*encellulement*' of medieval society.[74] Mills are therefore of central importance to our understanding of medieval landscapes (including monastic estates) and their management, especially since a mill's associated due, known as suit of mill (multure), was one whose pervasiveness and frequency of exaction made it a point of special anxiety for the local population. Technologically complex, mills also required a significant amount of investment, both in terms of initial construction and subsequent upkeep, such that they represented a constant source of dispute, settlement and (re-)negotiation across the medieval European map, including Normandy.[75] As Thomas Roche has recently noted, they were, therefore, a 'place' (*lieu*) in the landscape around which norms were negotiated and social hierarchies and physical boundaries defined, the study of which helps shed light on the ecclesiastical and secular networks within which an abbey operated and those which it mobilised.[76]

It is precisely these networks to which the three Mont Saint-Michel charters at the John Rylands Library bear witness. The first two, which have been mistakenly affixed into the Rylands album in reverse chronological order, deal with the consequences arising from the abbey's erection of a new mill at Carolles. Although the subsequent negotiations concerning this mill did not require the intervention of royal authority through the king's court, as was the case with disputes during this part of Abbot Jordan's reign in relation to the aforementioned Moulin-le-Comte, its construction nevertheless provoked a series of chain reactions in the locality, implicating a dozen individuals of various social ranks, all of whom were linked by feudal and/or familial bonds.[77] The first concerned the erection of the mill itself, which the first act, issued in the form of an undated chirograph charter-notice (Appendix, no. 1), tells us required the involvement of Nicholas de Verdun, with whom the monks had built the mill and its pond 'in common' (*communiter*). Once erected, a mill (as well as the distribution of its revenues, be it in grain or produce from its pond) relied, in part, on the control its owners exercised over members of the local population, to whom they granted rights for its exclusive use. The initial agreement negotiated to this effect under Abbot Jordan with regard to the new mill at Carolles therefore explicitly names those fiefs and men who depended upon it. Medieval mills were also the place in which the particular rights of the miller were established, with the same agreement stipulating that his installation at the new mill at Carolles was to take place 'by the common choice and consent' (*communi* [...] *electione et voluntate*) of the monks of Mont Saint-Michel and the lord of Verdun.

The fact that different individuals (or groups thereof) were associated with a mill regularly gave rise to tensions regarding the distribution of their rights and obligations both there and elsewhere in the vicinity. At Carolles, the new mill built 'in common' with Nicholas de Verdun soon began encroaching upon the workings of an older, neighbouring mill, thereby pushing nearly a dozen men, including Radulf de Carolles, to bring a complaint against the monks of Mont Saint-Michel. Interestingly, while Nicholas de Verdun is named at the beginning of the charter in the list of those in dispute with the abbey, the phrasing of the subsequent agreement, which is once again recorded in an undated chirograph charter-notice (Appendix, no. 2), seems to imply that the older mill did not belong to him, or to the abbey, but to the eleven individuals of lower social rank named alongside Nicholas, suggesting that what we have here is an example of a mill owned not by a lord (either ecclesiastical or secular) but by tenants.[78]

Whatever the case may be, the agreement negotiated in this regard under Abbot Jordan resulted in the division both of the revenues associated with these mills and the physical division of this part of the bay of Mont Saint-Michel. Circumscribing the abbey's authority to the area between the stream known as Le Crapeux and the sea, the agreement further divided the grain revenues between the three parties (the abbey, Nicholas de Verdun, the local men), and established their respective rights over the fishpond, the installation of the millers in both the old and new mills, and even access to pasture on the cliffs and banks where a plough could not furrow nor shelter be made.[79] A few years later, the third Rylands charter records how Reginald de Carolles confirmed the donation made to Mont Saint-Michel by his father Radulf, one of the claimants in the earlier suit who had subsequently become a monk there, of everything he possessed in the mills at Carolles and the nearby pond of La Cage. However, the fourteenth-century inventory reveals that it was necessary for the abbey to come to yet another agreement with Nicholas de Verdun in relation to the mill at Carolles, negotiated in 1219, the text of which is today unfortunately lost.[80] The resulting documentary landscape, of which the Rylands charters form a central part, is therefore one that opens a window on the ways in which mills were administered, both generally and in relation to the specific circumstances in the bay of Mont Saint-Michel, and on the complexity of the local customs surrounding them. Given the constant wrangling involved with their mill holdings, it is not surprising that many abbeys, suffering from litigious exhaustion, were prepared to transfer their mills in fief to local laymen, as Abbot Jordan did with the mill of Moulin-le-Comte in 1202.[81]

Conclusion

When viewed in isolation, the three Mont Saint-Michel charters now at the John Rylands Library (PHC/32–34) present little out of the ordinary. As noted, medieval mills were frequently the subject of disputes throughout the Middle Ages, while their role in the domination and division of the medieval landscape has long been a subject of study. However, it is the process by which this mechanism played out in practice with regard to Mont Saint-Michel and its wider estates that the destruction of the abbey's archives in 1944 renders obscure by comparison with many of its twelfth- and thirteenth-century contemporaries. The three Rylands charters studied, edited and translated here therefore stand as important witnesses to the ways in which Mont Saint-Michel and its abbots managed their possessions in the period either side of the loss of Normandy to the Capetians, from major assets located in far-flung territories down to a single yet highly valuable (and thus fiercely and repeatedly contested) watermill located a mere stone's throw from the abbey itself.

As rare originals, these acts can also be brought into fruitful conversation with other contemporary or near-contemporaneous documents, as well as with the abbey's fourteenth-century inventory, shedding light on the means by which the monks managed more than just their estates in the Middle Ages. Study of them here has thus not only helped contextualise both their endorsements and those found on surviving originals elsewhere, thereby allowing us to understand better the ways in which the monks of Mont Saint-Michel organised their now lost archives but may also encourage further work in this regard. Indeed, six of the Mont Saint-Michel charters today at the BnF are endorsed with a fifteenth-century note reading '*In registrata est*' (or something very similar).[82] Since only two of these acts are listed in the fourteenth-century inventory, it would seem that these notes refer to yet another document, perhaps a now lost inventory drawn up in the early fifteenth century when Abbot Pierre Le Roy is known to have been working with Mont Saint-Michel's archives, or perhaps to their inclusion in the lost cartulary or rental produced under his supervision. Whatever the case may be, just as the three Rylands charters are today but a tiny fragment of Mont Saint-Michel's lost archive, so the album in which they are now bound represents just one item in the enormous Phillipps collection of which it once formed a part, whose organisation, cultural-literary contexts, and usage by the wider scholarly community and emerging academy it reflects. Despite the near total destruction of Mont Saint-Michel's once enormous archive, there still remains much to be uncovered in relation to that which was seemingly lost to us on 6 June 1944, beginning with the hitherto little-known documents at the heart of this article.

Acknowledgements

The authors owe a debt of gratitude to John Hodgson, Associate Director (Curatorial Practices) at the John Rylands Research Institute and Library, and to Charlotte Denoël, Conservatrice en cheffe du service des manuscrits médiévaux at the Bibliothèque nationale de France, for their help in clarifying certain issues relating to some of the manuscripts in their respective care. They are also grateful to the two reviewers for their comments. Any errors that remain are their own.

Appendix

Editorial note. In the editions below, all abbreviated proper nouns are expanded using parentheses. Letters omitted by the scribe are provided by the editors in angled brackets (< >). In terms of orthography, 'u/v' and 'i/j' are kept as distinct vowels and consonants, respectively. In the translations, the modern canton and commune (when appropriate) is given for all identifiable place names, except those already identified in the main text above. Personal toponyms are preceded by 'de/du/de la' rather than 'of'.

1.

[1191 × 1212, and most probably 1191 × 1204].

A. Manchester, John Rylands Research Institute and Library, PHC/33. Endorsed: *Littera stagni et molend(ini) de* Carol(es) (s.xiii); *.LVI.* (s.xiv). Approx. 133 × 139 + 18 mm. Sealed *sur double queue, repli redoublé*, slits for one tag, tag and seal impression missing.

Inventory: no. 917.[88]

A

CYROGRAPHUM;   CYROGRAPHUM;

Scripto presenti[(a)] presentium memorie futurorumque noticie commendatur, quod cum[(b)] Jord(anus) abbas et monachi Montis |¹| sancti Mich(aelis) de periculo maris, ex una parte, et domnus Nich(olaus) de V(er)dum et heredes ejus, ex alia, haberent |²| locum aptum in dominicis suis ad construendum stagnum et molendinum, scilicet inter villa de *Karol(es)* et Sanctum |³| Clem(en)te(m), utroque concordia concurrente, fecerunt communiter stagnum et molendinum, ita quod dicti abbas et mo-|⁴|-nachi ad moltam ejusdem molendini continuo attornaverunt omnes homines quos tantum habebant,[(c)] et quos ha-|⁵|-bituri sunt, a torrente de *Crapout* usque ad mare, et in perpetuum concesserunt. Dictus vero Nich(olaus) et heredes ejus |⁶| similiter ad moltam ejusdem molendini attornaverunt omnes homines quos tantum habebant[(d)] et quos habituri sunt in feo-|⁷|-dis istis: in feodo Gellini de *Karol(es)*; in feodo Ansgot *Brient*; in feodo *Escollant*; in feodo Joh(ann)is de |⁸| Platea; in feodo Petri *Ansgot*; in feodo Will(elm)i *Picoul*, ubi manet; in feodo Hugonis de Capella, |⁹| et in perpetuum concesserunt, utpote qui de sua propria molta[(e)] erant. Et si abbas, monachi et dictus Nich(olaus) et heredes |¹⁰| ejus in confinio plures homines de sua molta rationabiliter habere poterunt, ad idem molendinum venire facient. |¹¹| Stagnum itaque et molendinum utriusque communia et omnes profectus qui de stagno et molendino poterunt prove-|¹²|-nire, inter eos per medium partientur. Sed et in opera et necessaria stagni et molendini mittent abbas et |13| monachi medietatem et sepedictus Nich(olaus) et heredes ejus aliam medietatem. Molendinarius etiam communi utriusque |14| partis electione et voluntate in molendino mittetur. Si autem quoquomodo molendinum per abbatem et monachos |15| vel per Nich(olaum) vel per heredes ejus molere non poterit, ille per cujus defectum molendinum jacuerit, alii tenebitur emen-|16|-dare super exitibus molendini qui ad eum pertinebunt. Hujus conditionis tenorem se servaturum in verbo Domini et |17| sacerdotis dixit abbas pro se et pro monachis sacrosanctum euuangelium tangendo et osculando, et sepedictus Nich(olaus) |18| super idem evangelium hoc ipsum juravit. Fulco etiam clericus, frater dicti Nich(olai), juravit hanc pactionem |19| se fideliter pro posse suo servaturum.

(a) presentu *corrected to* presenti *by erasure of final minim,* A. — (b) cum *inserted in interline,* A. — (c) hebebant *corrected to* habebant *by stroke on right side of first* e, A. — (d) hebebant, *sic* A. — (e) molltam *corrected to* moltam *by an expunging dot under the second* l, A.

Translation

CYROGRAPH;   ʹHdⱯꞪ⅁OꞄⱭↃ

With this present document notice is entrusted to the memory of those present and future that when Abbot Jordan and the monks of Mont Saint-Michel in peril of the sea, on the one side, and lord Nicholas de Verdun and his heirs, on the other, [have] had a suitable place in their demesnes for the construction of a pond and a mill, namely between the vill of Carolles and Saint-Clément,[89] they together built in mutually concurring agreement a pond and a mill, on condition that the said abbot and monks immediately attorned to the multure of the same mill all the men they so have and will have from the stream of Le Crapeux up to the sea, and have conceded [this] in perpetuity. The said Nicholas and his heirs have likewise attorned to the multure of the same mill all the men they so have and will have in these fiefs: the fief of Gellin de Carolles, the fief of Ansgot Brient, the Escollant fief, the fief of John de Platea, the fief of Peter Ansgot, the fief of William Picoul, where he lives, [and] the fief of Hugh de la Chapelle, and have conceded [this] in perpetuity, as if they were of their own multure. And if the abbot, monks, and the said Nicholas and his heirs are able reasonably to have more men of their multure in the neighbouring territory, they will make [them] go to the same mill. The pond and mill are therefore common to both, and all the proceeds that come forth from the pond and mill are to be shared between them in half. But of the works and needs of the pond and mill the abbot and monks will provide [one] half, and the aforesaid Nicholas and his heirs the other half. Moreover, the miller will be placed in the mill by the common choice and consent of both parties. If, however, the mill is in any way made unable to grind by the abbot and monks or by Nicholas and his heirs, he through whom the defective mill is inactive will be held to make amends to the other through the mill revenues that pertain to him. The abbot said he would keep the tenor of this agreement for himself and the monks, in the word of the Lord and of a priest, by touching and kissing the holy gospels, and the oft-mentioned Nicholas swore this thing on the same gospels. Fulk the clerk, brother of the said Nicholas,[90] also swore that he would faithfully keep this agreement to the best of his ability.

2.

[1191 × 1212, and most probably 1191 × 1204].

A. Manchester, John Rylands Research Institute and Library, PHC/32. Endorsed: [Litt]era concordiæ inter abbatem Mont(is) et Nich(olaum) de Verdun et participes (s.xiii);. VII. (s.xiv); [. . .]p[. . .] [m]olend[ini] de C(r)apot (s.xiv). Approx. 233 × 157 + 9 mm. Sealed *sur double queue, repli redoublé*, slits for two tags, tags and seal impressions missing.

Inventory: no. 971.

A

CYROGRAPHUM: :МUНPАЯ&ОЯYЭ

Noverint omnes ad quos presens scriptura pervenerit, quod cum longa contentio verteretur inter Jord(anum) abbatem et conventum Montis sancti Michaelis de periculo |¹| maris, ex una parte, et Nicholau(m) de V(er)dun, Rad(ulfum) de *Karoles*, Joh(ann)em *le Hungre*, Rog(erum) *Jolif*, Philipp(um) *Heudeart*, Rob(ertum) de G(r)antville, Ans-|²|-chetill(um) Malnorri, W. Malnorri, Rob(ertum) Malnorri, Rob(ertum) de Mota, Nich(olaum) filium P<h>ilippi, et Ric(ardum) de *Beslu(m)*, ex altera, super quodam molendino et viva-|³|-rio quod predictus abbas et Nich(olaus) de V(er)dun fecerant apud *Karoles*, et predicti homines in illis calumpniam faciebant, et super pastura quam idem Nich(olaus) |⁴| et homines sui super eumdem abbatem clamabant, tandem in hunc modum concordie pervenerunt: in illo siquidem molendino quod abbas et Nich(olaus) fe-|⁵|-cerant et in altero molendino quod primitus erat predictorum hominum percipient integre abbas et conventus terciam partem, prefatus Nich(olaus) de V(er)dun |⁶| terciam partem, et memorati homines terciam partem. Et similiter in omnibus emendatis que per illos communiter fient super illam aquam. Nec aliquis eo-|⁷|-rumdem quietus erit de moltura in illis molendinis. Primum tamen nominatum vivarium remanebit sepedictis abbati et Nich(olai) de *Verdun* cum omni pisca-|⁸|-ria et cum omnibus exitibus ejusdem vivarii. Predicti vero Nich(olaus) de V(er)dun et homines adducent totam moltam de parrochia de *Karoles* ad illa molendina et predicti |⁹| abbas et conventus totam moltam suam quam habent inter doitum de *C(r)apot* et mare adjacens. Predictis autem Nich(olao) de V(er)dun et hominibus remanebit pastura quam |¹⁰| ipsi clamabant super abbatem et conventum in falesiis et costilibus in quibus carrucca non poterit arare, vel ubi non poterit herbergagium fieri, et abbati |¹¹| similiter et conventui et hominibus suis remanebit pastura in falesiis et costilibus predictorum Nich(olai) et hominium suorum. In refactionibus vero et expen-|¹²|-sis oportebit mittere singulos ad terciam partem sicut ipsi percipiunt ad terciam partem. Unusquisque etiam tenetur cogere suam moltam venire ad predicta molen-|¹³|-dina. Et siquis eorum super hec defecerit, ad legitimam probationem reliquis partibus hec emendabit. Preterea molendinarii ponentur vel removebuntur |¹⁴| in illis molendinis per communuem assensum et consilium illarum trium partium. Testibus hiis: W. de *Leisels*, Oliv(er)o de *Leisels*, Ric(ardo) de *Leisels*, Guar(ino) |¹⁵| *Tyrel*, Fulc(one) de Bosco, Joh(ann)e *Malh(er)be*, Rann(ulfo) de *Guastign'*, W. de *Valleg(r)ente*, W. de Sancto Pet(r)o, Thom(e) de *Leisels*, Thom(e) de Bosco, |¹⁶| Fulc(one) de *Guastign'*, Rob(erto) de Mesnillo, Hugon(e) de *Boillon*, et multis aliis.

Translation

CYROGRAPH: :HdAЯGOЯYƆ

Let all those whom this present document may reach know that when a lengthy dispute arose between Abbot Jordan and the convent of Mont Saint-Michel in peril of the sea, on the one side, and Nicholas de Verdun, Radulf de Carolles, John le Hungre, Roger Jolif, Philip Heudeart, Robert de Granville,[91] Ansketil Malnorri, W. Malnorri, Robert Malnorri, Robert de *Mota*, Nicholas son of Philip, and Richard de *Beslum*, on the other, with regard to a certain mill and a fishpond that the aforesaid abbot and Nicholas de Verdun had built near Carolles, and about which the aforesaid men were making a claim, as well as with regard to the pasture that the same Nicholas and his men were claiming against the same abbot, they have at last come to an agreement in this form: indeed, in that mill which the abbot and Nicholas had built, and in the other mill that was originally that of the aforenamed men, the abbot and convent will receive a third part, in full, the aforesaid Nicholas a third part, and the aforesaid men a third part. And likewise [shall be shared] all the repairs made by them in common with regard to that water [i.e., the fishpond], nor will any of them be quit from multure in those mills. The aforenamed fishpond, however, along with all its fish and produce, will remain to the aforementioned abbot and Nicholas de Verdun. The aforenamed men and Nicholas de Verdun will take all the multure of the parish of Carolles to those mills, and the aforementioned abbot and convent will take [there] all the multure that they have between the stream of Le Crapeux and the adjacent sea. On the other hand, the pasture that the aforenamed men and Nicholas de Verdun were claiming against the abbot and convent will remain to them on the cliffs and banks where a plough cannot furrow, or where no shelter can be made, and likewise the pasture on the cliffs and banks of the aforementioned Nicholas and his men shall remain to the abbot and convent and their men. In repairs and expenses, however, it will be required for each to contribute a third part just as they receive a third part. Each [party] is also held to compel their multure to come to the aforesaid mills. And if any one of them falls short in this regard, he shall make amends to the other parties by legitimate proof. Moreover, the millers will be established or removed in these mills by the common consent and counsel of the three parties. With these witnesses: W. de Lézeaux,[92] Oliver de Lézeaux, Richard de Lézeaux, Warin Tirel, Fulk du Bois, John Malherbe, Rannulf de Gatigny,[93] W. du Vau Grante,[94] W. de Saint-Pierre, Thomas de Lézeaux, Thomas du Bois, Fulk de Gatigny, Robert du Mesnil, Hugh de Bouillon,[95] and many others.

3.

[?1216, 21 March.]—Avranches.

A. Manchester, John Rylands Research Institute and Library, PHC/34. Endorsed: [*Ca*]*rta Rag*(*inaldi*) *de Carolis de confirmatione donationis patris sui* (s.xiii); *.XIII.* (s.xiv). Approx. 200 × 154 + 34mm. Sealed *sur double queue, repli redoublé*, slit and four holes for cords, cords and seal impression missing.

Inventory: no. 978.

The witnesses Fulk de Gatigny, John Malherbe and Warin Tirel are all known to have been at the king's assize held at Avranches on 21 March 1216, which gives us the possible date of Reginald's charter.[96]

A

Omnibus ad quos presens scriptum pervenerit, Raginald(us) de Carolis, salutem. Noverit universitas vestra quod ego, pro salute |¹| anime mee et antecessorum meorum, dedi et concessi et confirmavi ecclesie beati Mich(ael)is de periculo maris et monachis ibidem |²| Deo servientibus, in puram et perpetuam elemosinam, quicquid Radulfus pater meus eidem ecclesie donavit quando mo-|³|-nachicum habitum suscepit, nichil inde mihi vel heredibus meis retinens, preter orationes ecclesie, videlicet quicquid ha-|⁴|-bebat in molendinis de Carolis. Dividuntur autem molendina illa in tres portiones, quarum altera ad predictam |⁵| ecclesiam pertinet, reliqua vero ad dominum meum Nicholaum de Verduno et ad heredes ejus. Tertia autem portione in |⁶| quatuor portiunculas divisa, dimidia pars trium portiuncularum ad prefatum patrem meum pertinebat, quam me-|⁷|-morate ecclesie in perpetuum integre possidendam concessit. Et preterea concessit eidem ecclesie situm stagni in Cagia, |⁸| in quantum terra sua protendebatur. Hanc siquidem donationem patris mei et concessionem meam concessit |⁹| et approbavit dominus Nicholaus de Verduno qui capitalis dominus est feodi in assisiis domini regis apud Abrinc(as). |¹⁰| Et ut hec donatio mea et concessio rata et irrevocabilis habeatur in posterum, presens scriptum sigilli mei muni-|[11]|-mine roboravi. Testibus: Radulfo *Herloin*, Philippo de Rupela, Will(el)mo de *Valgrente*, Garino *Tirel*, |[12]| Will(el)mo de *Leiseaus*, Olivero filio ejus, Hugone de *Boillon*, Fulcone de Gasteigni, Joh(ann)e *Malerbe*, |[13]| et multis aliis.

Translation

Reginald de Carolles [sends his] greeting to all whom this present document may reach. May you all know that I have given and conceded and confirmed, for the salvation of my soul and [the souls] of my ancestors, to the church of blessed Michael in peril of the sea and the monks who serve God there, in pure and perpetual alms, everything that my father Radulf gave to the same church when he accepted the monastic habit, namely, whatever he had in the mills of Carolles, retaining nothing for myself or my heirs, except the church's prayers. Those mills are now divided in three parts, another one of which belongs to the aforesaid church [and] the remaining [one] to my lord, Nicholas de Verdun, and his heirs. The third part [is] divided into four smaller parts, however. Half of three smaller parts pertained to my aforementioned father, which he conceded to the [afore]mentioned church to be held wholly, in perpetuity. And he also conceded to the same church the site of the pond at La Cage,[97] insofar as it extended in his land. Nicholas de Verdun, who is the chief lord of the fief, has since conceded and endorsed this my father's donation and my concession in the lord king's assizes at Avranches. And so that this my donation and concession remain valid and irreversible in the future, I have reinforced the present document with the strength of my seal. With [these] witnesses: Radulf Herloin, Philip de la Rochelle, William du Vau Grante, Warin Tirel, William de Lézeaux, his son Oliver, Hugh de Bouillon, Fulk de Gatigny, John Malherbe, and many others.

Notes

1 Manche, cant. Avranches.
2 The foundation of Mont Saint-Michel is recited in a legendary text known as the *Revelatio ecclesiæ sancti Michaelis*, which was written, in all likelihood, in the early ninth century. For discussion, along with a critical edition and translation, see P. Bouet and O. Desbordes, *Chroniques latines du Mont Saint-Michel (IXe–XIIe siècle)* (Caen: Presses universitaires de Caen, 2009), pp. 29–103; also P. Bouet and O. Desbordes, *Le Mont Saint-Michel: Enluminures et textes fondateurs* (Rennes: Éditions Ouest-France, 2018), pp. 20–37. Not everyone agrees with the early ninth century date, however. For a summary of the debate, see I. Rosé, 'Fondations et réformes à l'époque carolingienne', in *Monachesimi d'oriente e d'occidente nell'alto medioevo* (Spoleto, 31 marzo-6 aprile 2016), 2 vols (Spoleto: Fondazione Centro italiano di studi sull'alto Medioevo, 2017), I, pp. 397–462, at p. 452, n. 183.

3   The 205 manuscripts from the abbey's medieval library now housed at Avranches were digitised in the early 2000s. These images, along with catalogue descriptions, can today be consulted online via the *Bibliothèque virtuelle du Mont Saint-Michel*: https://emmsm.unicaen.fr/emmsm/bvmsm/accueil.html [accessed 30 July 2023].

4   For a description of what was destroyed on 6 June 1944, with estimates of numbers, see Y. Nédélec, 'Répertoire des bibliothèques et archives de la Manche', *Revue du département de la Manche*, 4 (1962), 357–441, at 395. For a preliminary survey of what survives, see M. Bisson, 'Où sont les archives du Mont Saint-Michel?', in P. Bauduin *et al.* (eds), *Sur les pas de Lanfranc, du Bec à Caen: Recueil d'études en hommage à Véronique Gazeau* (Caen: Annales de Normandie, 2018), pp. 453–63.

5   For further discussion, see R. Allen, 'Le chartrier perdu du Mont Saint-Michel: réseaux, échanges et construction spatiale dans le diocèse d'Avranches (XIe–XIIIe s.)', in F. Paquet and M. Labatut (eds), *1023–2023. Le Mont Saint-Michel en Normandie et en Europe. Nouvelles découvertes et nouvelles perspectives de recherche* (Actes du colloque de Cerisy-la-Salle, 31 mai–4 juin 2023) (Caen: Presses universitaires de Caen, forthcoming).

6   The only other study to discuss these three charters, alongside others, in the specific context of their physical preservation and compilation is B. Pohl, 'Scholarly Pursuit or *Sammelwut*? (Re-)Framing Medieval Manuscripts in Two Nineteenth-Century Albums (Bristol Archives, 08153/1, and Manchester, University Library–John Rylands Research Library, PHC/28–67)', in S. Brähler *et al.* (eds), *Memorial Volume for Prof. Dr. Christoph Houswitschka* (Bamberg: University of Bamberg Press, 2024), pp. 195–214.

7   On Phillipps and Middle Hill, see A. Munby, *Portrait of an Obsession: The Life of Sir Thomas Phillipps, the World's Greatest Book Collector* (London: Constable, 1967); more recently C. De Hamel, *The Posthumous Papers of the Manuscripts Club* (London: Allen Lane, 2022), pp. 339–43.

8   *Phillippica: Catalogue of a Further Portion of the Classical, Historical, Topographical, Genealogical and Other Manuscripts and Autograph Letters of the Late Sir Thomas Phillipps. 6–9 June 1910* (London: Sotheby, Wilkinson & Hodge, 1910), p. 34 (lot 186).

9   R. Fawtier, 'Hand-Lists of Charters and Deeds in the Possession of the John Rylands Library. IV. The Phillipps Charters', *Bulletin of the John Rylands Library*, 8:2 (1924), 456–508, at 472; R. Fawtier, *Hand-List of Charters, Deeds, and Similar Documents in the Possession of the John Rylands Library*, 3 vols (Manchester: Manchester University Press, 1925–37), I, p. 57.

10 T. Burrows, '"There Never Was Such a Collector Since the World Began": A New Look at Sir Thomas Phillipps', in T. Burrows and C. Johnston (eds), *Collecting the Past: British Collectors and Their Collections from the 18th to the 20th Centuries* (London: Routledge, 2018), pp. 45–62, at p. 45.

11 The number is manually inscribed, in ink, on the inside of its front cover, with the 'sister album', PHC/68–125, carrying the manuscript number 32,289 in the same place. On Phillipps's custom of numbering and inscribing his books, see A. Munby, *The Catalogues of Manuscripts and Printed Books of Sir Thomas Phillipps* (Cambridge: Cambridge University Press, 1951), pp. 1–17.

12 On the complexities of the Phillipps catalogue, see R. Folter, 'Catalogues of the Library of Sir Thomas Phillipps: A Chronological Checklist', in J.H. Marrow *et al.* (eds), *The Medieval Book: Glosses from Friends and Colleagues of Christopher De Hamel* ('t Goy-Houten: Hes & De Graaf, 2010), pp. 355–65.

13 For these inventories, see Burrows, '"Never Such a Collector"', p. 50.

14 A note in one of the Phillipps-Robinson manuscripts contains a list of manuscripts, including those of the twelfth and thirteenth centuries, which Phillipps 'bought in France between 1827 & 1830, but [which] were left with many printed books in [the] care of old Mr de Rheims of Calais untill [*sic*] I returned home to Middle Hill, but he & and his son detained them until the year 1859, during which time (near 30 years) he had put them on his own shelves & enjoyed the use of them, & then wanted me to pay for keeping them': Oxford, Bodleian Libraries (hereafter OBL), MS Phillipps-Robinson d. 309, fol. 36r.

15 Fenwick, whose mother had been left the whole of Phillipps's library, rationalised parts of his grandfather's collection and continued numbering up to 38,628: A. Munby, *The Formation of the Phillipps Library from 1841 to 1872* (Cambridge: Cambridge University Press, 1956), p. 166.

16 Burrows, '"Never Such a Collector"', p. 50.

17 OBL, MSS Phillipps-Robinson b. 207–15, c. 670–92, c. 696, d. 288–312, d. 323–5, e. 456–77, f. 72–82.

18 For recent discussion, see Pohl, 'Scholarly Pursuit or *Sammelwut*?'; M. Connolly, 'The Album and the Scrapbook', *Florilegium*, 35 (2018), 31–51.

19 'Carta Andrea abbatis S. Stephani de Bosco, a[nn]o 1240, Rogero de Amica, imperiali capitaneo. In a black case. fol. V. s. xiii': OBL, MS Phillipps-Robinson c. 678, fol. 33r. The charter was accorded the manuscript number 22,768 in the final part of the catalogue published in 1871: *Catalogus librorum manuscriptorum in bibliotheca d. Thomæ Phillipps, bart.* (Impressum Typis in Medio-Montanis, 1837–71), p. 421.

20 OBL, MS Phillipps-Robinson d. 297, fol. 33r.

21 The list is to be found in OBL, MS Phillipps-Robinson c. 679, fol. 87r-v, as follows:

<u>Catalogue of ancient charters at Middle Hill, 1848</u>
1. Bulla p. Alexandri abbati Silvæ Marjoris Burdegal, 15 kal nov.
2. Carta Frumaldi Atrebatens. ministri de redditibus de Raisa, AD 1181.
3. Ditto Ademari Xanton. episcopi de ecclesia B.M. de Insula.
4. Ditto Bertranni Mettens. episcopi de patronatu Gaufridi de Asperomonte in ecclesia de Sivereio. AD 1200.
5. Ditto Frederici ducis de Bites abbatis [*sic*] Vallis S. Mariæ de Sturceleburnan de ecclesiis Walespure et Werde. AD 1196.
6. Ditto Bertrammi Mettensis episcopi Willelmo abbate [*sic*] S. Vincentii (de Metz) et Richero presbytero de vicario sancti Germani de ecclesia de Castello. AD 1181.
7. Ditto Gosleni Suessorum episcopi Petro abbati Cluniacensis monasterii pro ecclesia Consiacensi de ecclesiis S. Petri de Calce, Bruellio, S. M. de Cruce Spalt [?], Estrepilli, Terri [?] Wesli, Masiaco, Roothcurte, Cartobrio, Hermentario et Curtfabro. AD 1139.

8. Ditto Symonis Noviomensis episcopi de ecclesia de Valle Secreta in territorio de Fillanis. AD 1143. [Genealogical tree of Robert de Fillanis and his wife Elizabeth]
9. Bulla Alex[and]ri papæ … decano et canonicis sancti Quintini. Dat. Anagniæ 4 kal. junii.
10. Carta Roberti decani Laudunensis de vinea dicta Les Perchies. AD 1186. [Genealogical tree of five brothers: Hugo de Hayles, Drogo, Albert, Everard and Morisius]
11. Ditto Lamberti de Masereh et Thom. filii ejus pro ecclesia S. M. de Wauera quo est cella S. Petri de Haffligem. AD 1125.
12. Ditto Rotberti de Sablullio et Hazuisa uxor. ejus dat. S. Martini Majoris Monasterii ecclesiam S. Macuti, cum confirmatione Philippi regis Francorum dum esset ipse rex in obsidione castelli Calvimontis. Circa AD 1080. [Genealogical tree of Robert de Sablullio and his wife Hazuisa]
13. Ditto Desiderii Morinorum episcopi Roberto abbati Liskensis de ecclesia de Liskis in qua Milo Morinensis episcopus ordinavit abbatiam Ecchis [?]. Data 1170.
14. Carta Hel. Burdegal archiepiscopi pro abb. Silvae Majoris. AD 1196.
15. Ditto Nivelonis Suessionens episcopi de donationæ ecclesiæ S. Johannis de Vineis per Galterum Cathalancensem et Pentecosten uxorem ejus et eorum filios Theodosium et Galterum. AD 1197.
16. Ditto Theoderici electi Mettensis Mathildi abbatissæ sancti Petri Mettensis de ecclesia S. Viti in Mettensi. AD 1176.
17. Ditto Hugonis Cluniacnesis abbatis de fundacione de Marcigny. AD 1102.
18. Ditto Alberonis Trevirorum episcopi Ebembardo abbati S. Vincenti (Mettensis) de ecclesia S. Germani de Castollo. AD 1141.
19. Ernaldis Cenomannensium abbati de S. Martino Maioris monasterii, confirmat ecclesias sancti Guingualoei, Vivonium, Valle Guidonis et locum S. Macuti de Sablolio. Dat. AD 1068.
20. Testamentum Johannis Cruel granting donations to the town of Lens. No date but sæc. XII.
21. Carta Manassis Suessor. episcopi de altari villæ de Lostria dato ecclesiæ S. Johannis. Circa 1080.
22. Bulla p. Alexandri 3^{tii} anno VI Roberto abbati S. Mar de Liskes. AD 1164.
23. Ditto p. Alexandri 3 anno V Petro abbati S. Mar Silvæ Majoris. AD 1163.

22 In the list above, the following charters are found in the Paris manuscript. 1 (= BnF, MS nouv. acq. lat. 2588, no. 13); 2 (= *ibid.*, no. 14); 3 (= *ibid.*, no. 15); 11 (= *ibid.*, no. 4); 12 (= *ibid.*, no. 2); 13 (= *ibid.*, no. 10); 14 (= *ibid.*, no. 16); 17 (= *ibid.*, no. 3); 19 (= *ibid.*, no. 1); 20 (= *ibid.*, no. 18); 22 (= *ibid.*, no. 8); 23 (= *ibid.*, no. 7).
23 H. Omont, *Catalogue des manuscrits latins et français de la Collection Phillipps acquis en 1908 pour la Bibliothèque nationale* (Paris: E. Leroux, 1909), pp. i, viii, and 95–9, no. XCV.
24 For Phillipps's travels to France, see A. Munby, *The Formation of the Phillipps Library up to the Year 1840* (Cambridge: Cambridge University Press, 1954), pp. 19–41.
25 BnF, MS nouv. acq. lat. 2588, nos 1, 3, 7–8.

26 *Ibid.*, no. 12 (= 26,098); nos 21, 23, 59, 63, 75 (= 25,104); nos 27, 83, 86 (= 25,674); nos 48, 76bis (= 27,928); no. 73 (= 27,015); no. 94 (= 25,098).

27 *Ibid.*, no. 17 (= 33,812). It is possible that no. 38 has the same number on its reverse, of which only the first two digits are visible, the others being obscured by the way in which the act has been pasted into the volume.

28 For example, *ibid.*, nos 57, 85, 95–8 all have the Phillipps number 17,089 on their reverse. In contrast, the corresponding number in the catalogue is among those manuscripts acquired from William Monk Mason's Dublin collection, where it is described as 'Bearla Feine *sm. 4tor ch. s. xviii, brn.cf. gt*': *Catalogus librorum Phillipps*, p. 329. The same is true for BnF, MS nouv. acq. lat. 2588, nos 25 (= 18,676), 30 (= 22,305), nos 41, 74, 77 (= 22,309), nos 42, 44-45, 55 (= 23,113), and nos 60–61, 67 (= 23,115), while no. 52 (= 23,114) is described correctly.

29 While some charters have been bound into the Paris manuscript so that their reverse is entirely visible, many have been pasted directly onto the album's paper pages. Small windows have been cut so that medieval and early modern endorsements are visible, but certain Phillipps numbers are either partially obscured (see n. 27) or, in some instances, presumably completely hidden from sight.

30 For much of what follows and further discussion, see Pohl, 'Scholarly Pursuit or *Sammelwut*?'

31 De Hamel, *Posthumous Papers*, pp. 321–3.

32 OBL, MS Phillipps-Robinson c. 679, fos 36r–41v.

33 This was the case with another German medievalist, Theodor Mommsen (1817–1903), who visited Cheltenham at the invitation of Thomas Fitzroy Fenwick to study (and subsequently publish) selected manuscripts from Phillipps's vast library: De Hamel, *Posthumous Papers*, pp. 400–1. On Phillipps's other visitors, see Munby, *Formation up to 1840*, pp. 138–42; Munby, *Formation from 1841 to 1872*, pp. 29–42 and 86–93.

34 For a full list of the large private collections bought by Phillipps between 1824 and 1869/70, see Burrows, '"Never Such a Collector"', p. 46.

35 For de la Rue, see N. Vincent, *Norman Charters from English Sources: Antiquaries, Archives and the Rediscovery of the Anglo-Norman Past* (London: Pipe Roll Society, 2013), pp. 72–5. For some other Norman charters that eventually made their way to the John Rylands Library via Gervase de la Rue, see L. Gathagan, 'Abbess, Judge, Jailor: Authority and Imprisonment at Holy Trinity, Caen', *Bulletin of the John Rylands Library*, 99:2 (2023), 25–46.

36 Phillipps acquired two Bayeux cartularies from de la Rue's library, which became Phillipps MSS 10,337 and 21,709 (*Catalogus librorum Phillipps*, pp. 166, 403). These manuscripts were subsequently acquired by the BnF, where they are now MSS nouv. acq. lat. 925 and 926.

37 An original charter of 1237 (n.s.) can be found today pasted into a manuscript with copies of Mont Saint-Michel acts made by or for François Roger de Gaignières (1642–1715): BnF, MS lat. 5430A, p. 294.

38 For Jeremiah Wiffen, who acquired two Mont Saint-Michel charters now at the British Library, see N. Vincent, 'A Collection of Early Norman Charters in the British Library: The Case of Jeremiah Holmes Wiffen', *Cahiers Léopold Delisle*, 53 (2004), 21–45, at

26–30. The Mont Saint-Michel charters in BnF, MS lat. 9215, on which more below, may also have been extracted from the archives at Saint-Lô at this time.

39 Avranches, Bibliothèque municipale (hereafter ABM), MS 210. A modern edition of the cartulary's twelfth-century portion can be found in K. S. B. Keats-Rohan (ed.), *The Cartulary of the Abbey of Mont-Saint-Michel* (Donington: Shaun Tyas, 2006).

40 B. Pohl, 'L' « atelier historique » de l'abbé-historien Robert de Torigni: où a-t-il écrit?', in Paquet and Labatut (eds), *1023–2023. Le Mont Saint-Michel*.

41 P. Gout, *Le Mont-Saint-Michel: histoire de l'abbaye et de la ville: étude archéologique et architecturale des monuments*, 2 vols (Paris: Libraire Armand Colin, 1910), II, p. 535. Others have retained the 1406 date but have argued that Pierre Le Roy was responsible not necessarily for building the tower but instead for fitting it out or remodelling it: M. Reulos, 'L'organisation et l'administration de l'abbaye à partir de l'abbé Pierre le Roi jusqu'à l'application du Concordat', in J. Laporte et al. (eds), *Millénaire monastique du Mont Saint-Michel*, 5 vols (Paris: P. Lethielleux, 1967–2001), I, pp. 191–209, at p. 194.

42 'In armariolo privilegiorum. In subsequentibus signatur littere efficaces contente in armariolis cartarii, et pro de armariolo in quo privilegia apostolica continentur': ABM, MS 211, fol. 113v.

43 N. Simon, 'Le Mont Saint-Michel dans les trois prémiers quarts du XIVe siècle', in Laporte et al. (eds), *Millénaire monastique*, I, pp. 151–90, at pp. 152–60.

44 Reulos, 'L'organisation et l'administration', p. 204. On the *Livre blanc*, see Keats-Rohan (ed.), *Cartulary*, pp. 31–2. For the *Quanandrier*, see Reulos, 'L'organisation et l'administration', p. 193.

45 ABM, MS 211, fos 113v–137r. A transcription can be found in C. Coutant, 'Le cartulaire de l'abbaye du Mont-Saint-Michel et ses additions. Étude et édition critique' (unpublished thesis, l'École des chartes, Paris, 2009), pp. 150–217.

46 'Hec extractio facta fuit anno Domini M^o CCC^o vicesimo VI° die martis post octavam nativitatis Beate Marie virginis per aliquos fratres de istius et quorum multa in continentur forte inutilia vel defectiva in aliquo ipsi rogant legentes ut eos habeant excusatos nam ipsi collegerunt harum cyrographarum seu cartarum istarum breviter pro ut melius potuere': ABM, MS 211, fol. 137v.

47 There is an act of 1341 ('LX. Littera quod Philippe de *Rouel* quitavit unum mercatum burse factum cum Martino de Vincelois ratione uxoris sue, videlicet de II quarteriis frumenti cum Johanne de Dolo, Johanne *Gelin* et Hamone *Letecense*. MCCCXLI.': *ibid.*, fol. 130r), and another of 1381 ('XXXVII. Littera regis facta per Johan relictam *au noteor de Dragé* de VI s. redditus cum Guillemo *Coston* super peciam terre *a la Bequemie*. MCCCLXXXI.': *ibid.*, fol. 130v).

48 For much of what follows, see Allen, 'Le chartrier perdu'.

49 Manche, cant. Granville.

50 For the note at the beginning, see n. 42. The second note, which is underlined and appears next to the entry for an act of Richard II, duke of Normandy (996–1026), instructs those interested 'to look in the chest/cupboard of the Mont' ('Quere in armariolo Montis': ABM, MS 211, fol. 120), which suggests that it had been moved from

the Saint-Pair chest/cupboard to be alongside the abbey's other ducal acts kept in the '*armariolum Montis*'.

51 Keats-Rohan (ed.), *Cartulary*, p. 40.

52 'Littera Gervasii filii Hehie [*sic*] de pistrino de Genez. MCLXVI.' and 'Cyrographum Gervasii filii Helie de excambio pistrini de Genez. MCLXVI.': ABM, MS 211, fos 127v and 128r.

53 Auffains, Eure-et-Loir, cant. Les Villages Vovéens, com. Éole-en-Beauce. For a critical edition of Reginald's act, see Coutant, 'Le cartulaire', no. 82, pp. 284–5.

54 PHC/32 is one half of a chirograph. It would seem that the abbey's archives also possessed the other half, since the fourteenth-century inventory contains another entry that describes its contents precisely: 'Littera vivarii et molendini de *Karoles* quod habeamus terciam partem, Nicholaus du *Verdun* aliam et plures alii aliam partem. Non quotatur': ABM, MS 211, fol. 128v.

55 See the finding aid *1 H – Fonds de l'abbaye du Mont-Saint-Michel. Épaves des archives de l'abbaye du Mont-Saint-Michel* (Saint-Lô: Archives de la Manche, undated), p. 2: https://www.archives-manche.fr/_depot_ad50/_depot_fonds/inventaires/ancien/1_H.pdf [accessed 2 July 2023].

56 These charters are today bound into a composite volume containing original acts from other Norman religious institutions (BnF, MS lat. 9215). Those relating to the Cistercian abbey of Aunay were acquired from Denis Désiré Riocreux (1791–1872), director of the museum of Sèvres: L. Delisle, *Le cabinet des manuscrits de la Bibliothèque impériale*, 4 vols (Paris: Impr. impériale [puis] nationale, 1868–81), II, p. 289. He does not appear to have been behind the donation of the Mont Saint-Michel acts, however, which Léopold Delisle's unpublished *Inventaire des chartes. Fonds latins*, pp. 375–81 seems to suggest arrived at the BnF in two parts (http://catalogue.bnf.fr/ark:/12148/cb42195807m [accessed 2 July 2023]). This collection of 36 acts, one of which was repurposed as a powder cartridge, most likely escaped the abbey's archives before the French Revolution or in its very immediate aftermath.

57 The only endorsement visible today on the Paris charter is from the fifteenth century. That said, the charter has been affixed into the album in which it is now found in such a way as to render part of the reverse illegible. It is therefore possible that an earlier endorsement has been obscured. The inventory entry has been numbered by a fifteenth-century scribe, possibly Abbot Pierre Le Roy (see, p. 18), using an Arabic numeral, which may also have been obscured along with an earlier endorsement. Modern copies do show, however, that not every Mont Saint-Michel act had a medieval endorsement (or only had them from the fifteenth century). See, for example, R. Allen, 'Unknown Copies of the Lost Charters of Le Mont Saint-Michel (11th–13th c.): The Henry Chanteux Collection at the Archives départementales du Calvados', *Revue Mabillon*, 29 (2018), 45–82, at Appendix II, nos 2, 7 and 9, 75, 79–80.

58 Unlike the charters in the abbey's cartulary described by the inventory as chirographs, this charter, now in the British Library, is an actual chirograph, two copies of which were once kept in the monastic archives. These are both described in the inventory, one after the other. Since the first entry describes the charter in terms not found on the reverse of the surviving original in London, we can reasonably conclude that this

charter is the one described by the inventorist in curtailed form ('Item alia sub eodem tenore. MCXXI': ABM, MS 211, fol. 128v). Another original with an endorsement that uses the term '*cirographum*' is now among the handful of Mont Saint-Michel originals at Saint-Lô (Saint-Lô, Archives départementales de la Manche (hereafter ADM), 1 H 7: 'Cirographum pro furno sancti Johannis et prato apud Milleciam'). At first glance, this would appear not to be a strict chirograph since it contains neither a device in its margins nor shows any sign of being indented. Its twin, however, survives as ADM, 1 H 8. It has the device 'CIROGRAPHUM' across its upper margin but is described in the only endorsement as 'De furno in parrochia sancti Johannis juxta furnum nostrum et de prato apud Mileciam'. It would appear, therefore, that the top edge of the first of these charters has been trimmed. These acts are not listed in the inventory.

59 The sections with numbers next to their entries are as follows: 'Dona et confirmationes regis Francorum et ducis Normannorum factum et datum abbatie Montis sanctis Michaelis' [fol. 114r, Arabic]; 'Emptiones' [fol. 114v, Arabic]; 'Ardevon' [fos 115r–116r, Arabic]; 'Sanctus Paternus' [fos 120r–122r, Roman]; 'Genez' [fos 127r–128v, Roman]; 'Saint Jehan de Thomas' [fol. 128v, Roman]; 'Pitancia' [fos 129r–132v, largely Roman with some Arabic]; and 'Mons Rouaudi' [fol. 133r, Arabic].

60 Manche, cant. Ponterson.

61 This is the section in which the papal bulls are listed: ABM, MS 211, fol. 113v.

62 Besides the royal/ducal acts and purchases, the remaining sections contain the following number of acts: Ardevon (113 acts), Saint-Pair (228 acts), Genêts and Saint-Jean-le-Thomas (130 acts), and Pitances (212 acts). The exception is the section for Mont Rouault (Ille-et-Vilaine, cant. Dol-de-Bretagne, com. Pleine-Fougères), which contains only 24 acts.

63 M. Hagger, *The Fortunes of a Norman Family: The de Verduns in England, Ireland, and Wales, 1066–1316* (Dublin: Four Courts Press, 2001), p. 60; Vincent, 'Jeremiah Wiffen', 23 n. 6; Vincent, *Norman Charters*, p. 78 n. 277.

64 BnF, MS lat. 5430A (Gaignières); *ibid*., MS lat. 10072 and Kew, The National Archives, PRO 31/8/140B (d'Anisy); BnF, MS nouv. acq. fr. 21821–21822 (Delisle).

65 Allen, 'Unknown Copies', 45–82. See also Allen, 'Le chartrier perdu'.

66 Robert's immediate successor, Martin de Furmendi, was abbot only for around three and a half years. Very little is known of his abbacy: V. Gazeau, *Normannia monastica*, 2 vols (Caen: Publications du CRAHM), II, pp. 225–6. On the imposing memory of Robert of Torigni's abbacy at Mont Saint-Michel and beyond, see B. Pohl, 'The Memory of Robert of Torigni: From the Twelfth Century to the Present Day', in F. Paquet (ed.), *Maîtriser le temps et façonner l'histoire. Les historiens normands aux époques médiévale et moderne* (Caen: Presses universitaires de Caen, 2022), pp. 111–34; B. Pohl, 'Robert of Torigni and Le Bec: The Man and the Myth', in B. Pohl and L. Gathagan (eds), *A Companion to the Abbey of Le Bec in the Central Middle Ages (11th–13th Centuries)* (Leiden: Brill, 2017), pp. 94–124.

67 J. Chazelas, 'La vie monastique au Mont Saint-Michel au XIIIe siècle', in Laporte *et al.* (eds), *Millénaire monastique*, I, pp. 127–50, at p. 140–3; M. Nortier, 'La construction de la Merveille. Nouvelle datation proposée', in *ibid.*, V, pp. 81–96, at p. 84.

68 Allen, 'Unknown Copies', Appendix I, no. 74, 70 (an act of Guimond, prior of Mont Saint-Michel, issued 'cum precepto et voluntate donni Jordani abbatis', which is mistakenly attributed by Allen to Abbot Jordan), Mont Rouault, Ille-et-Vilaine, cant. Dol-de-Bretagne, com. Pleine-Fougères; P. de Farcy, *Cartulaire de Saint-Victeur au Mans, prieuré de l'abbaye du Mont-Saint-Michel (994–1400)* (Paris: A. Picard et fils, 1895), pp. 29–31, no. XXVIII.

69 Allen, 'Le chartrier perdu', Annexe, no. 7. Bacilly, Manche, cant. Avranches.

70 On the family of Verdun (Manche, cant. and com. Pontorson), and on Nicholas in particular, see Hagger, *The Fortunes*, pp. 59–71.

71 For recent discussion in an English context, see A. Lucas, *Ecclesiastical Lordship, Seigneurial Power and the Commercialization of Milling in Medieval England* (Farnham: Ashgate, 2014).

72 The Premonstratensian abbey of La Lucerne, for example, had mills at places such as Saint-Pierre-Langers, Saint-Jean-le-Thomas, and Sartilly (all Manche, cant. Avranches), to name but a few, which were located within a seven-kilometre radius of Carolles. For discussion, see D. Ducœur, 'Les moulins de l'abbaye de La Lucerne', *Revue de l'Avranchin et du pays de Granville*, 84 (2007), 223–84, at 227–9.

73 D. Pichot, 'Le moulin et l'encellulement dans l'Ouest français (XIe–XIIIe siècle)', in M. Mousnier (ed.), *Moulins et meuniers dans les Campagnes européennes (IXe–XVIIIe siècle)* (Toulouse: Presses universitaires du Midi, 2002), pp. 110–29, at p. 122.

74 R. Fossier, *L'enfance de l'Europe, Xe–XIIe siècles: aspects économiques et sociaux*, 2 vols (Paris: Presses universitaires de France, 1982), I, pp. 288–595.

75 See, for example, the agreement reached between Abbot William (II) of Saint-Étienne de Caen (1156–81) and one Radulf of Cairon (Calvados, cant. Bretteville-l'Orgueilleuse) concerning a jointly-held mill in *Bauduchonville*, evidence of which survives in the abbey's twelfth-century cartulary as well as in an original charter now kept at the British Library in London: B. Pohl, 'Eight Twelfth-Century Charters from the Norman Abbey of Saint-Étienne de Caen, *c.*1120–1204 (London, British Library, Add. Chs. 67574–67581) – A Catalogue and Commentary', *Electronic British Library Journal* (2017), 1–52, at 9–10 (edition and translation) and 26–27 (discussion); the mill of *Bauduchonville* was confirmed to the abbot and monks of Saint-Étienne, along with all other mills the monastery held within the diocese of Bayeux, by Archbishop Rotrou of Rouen (1165–84): B. Pohl, 'Processions, Power and Public Display: Ecclesiastical Rivalry and Ritual in Ducal Normandy,' *Journal of Medieval Monastic Studies*, 6 (2017), 1–49, at 39.

76 T. Roche, 'Les moines de Jumièges et les moulins de Montataire', in D. Hanquiez and A. Petit (eds), *Saint-Leu-d'Esserent et l'implantation monastique dans la basse vallée de l'Oise* (Actes du colloque de Saint-Leu-d'Esserent, 27–29 octobre 2011) (Amiens: CAHMER, Laboratoire d'archéologie, Université de Picardie, 2012), pp. 37–58.

77 For discussion, see Allen, 'Le chartrier perdu'.

78 Although mills are commonly associated with peasants' obligations to their lords, some were held by tenants: G. White, *The Medieval English Landscape, 1000–1540* (London: Bloomsbury, 2012), p. 51.
79 The Crapeux flows from its source in the village of Saint-Michel-des-Loups (Manche, cant. Avranches, com. Jullouville) to the sea.
80 'VI. Carta Nicholai de Verduno de molendino de *Karoles*, videlicet de compositione acta inter nos et ipsum. MCCXIX. Alia non quotatur': ABM, MS 211, fol. 128v.
81 Allen, 'Le chartrier perdu'.
82 BnF, MS lat. 9215, nos 69 ('In registr(ata) [e]st'); 70 ('Inregestrata'); 80 ('In regist(rata) est'); 81 ('In registrata est'); 82 ('In regist(ra)ta est'); 83 ('In registrata est').
83 It would seem that there were two copies of this charter conserved in the abbey's archives (see above, n. 55).
84 Although the verb *quotare* literally means 'to mark with numerical reference' (R. Latham, D. Howlett and R. Ashdowne (eds), *Dictionary of Medieval Latin from British Sources* (London: Oxford University Press for the British Academy, 1975–2013), fasc. 13. Pro-Reg, p. 2642), the inventorist appears to use '*non quotatur*' throughout to mean 'not dated'.
85 Sadly, three thirteenth-century Mont Saint-Michel charters in this manuscript (nos 75–6, 78) have been affixed to the page in such a way as to render the reverse illegible.
86 The final words of this endorsement are hidden by the way this charter has been affixed into this album. It is possible the Roman numeral 'XI', which is found in the inventory entry, has also been obscured in this way.
87 An asterisk denotes when the modern copy does not specifically identify this text, which is almost always found at the head of the transcription, as an endorsement.
88 This number is that assigned to the corresponding entry in Coraline Coutant's transcription of the fourteenth-century inventory.
89 The place called Saint-Clément was home to a hospital, which an agreement of 1232 shows was reserved exclusively for the use of leprous monks of Mont Saint-Michel: Allen, 'Unknown Copies', Appendix I, no. 13, 61. Its precise location is difficult to determine, although it was likely towards the cliffs of Carolles near the place now known as the Rocher du Sard: E.-A. Pigeon, *Le diocèse d'Avranches, sa topographie, ses origines, ses évêques, sa cathédrale, ses églises, ses comtes et ses châteaux*, 2 vols (Coutances: Salettes, 1888), I, p. 105.
90 Fulk is a previously unknown member of the de Verdun family.
91 Manche, chef-lieu de cant.
92 Either Manche, cant. Avranches, com. Jullouville or Manche, cant. Granville, com. Saint-Pair-sur-Mer.
93 Manche, cant. Granville, com. Saint-Pair-sur-Mer.
94 Manche, cant. Isigny-le-Buat, com. Tirepied-sur-Sée.
95 Manche, cant. Avranches, com. Jullouville.
96 Coutant, 'Le cartulaire', no. 128, pp. 324–5.
97 Manche, cant. Avranches, com. Carolles.

Peter Legh and the Electoral Management of Newton, 1685–1744

RICHARD HARRISON, UNIVERSITY OF YORK

Abstract

The nature of Britain's unreformed parliamentary electoral system has been the focus of interest and study for over two centuries. For the unreformed period, historians have identified a range of factors influencing the outcome of parliamentary elections: prevailing economic and social power structures; the nature, extent and effectiveness of electoral treating and corruption; and the role of political issues, among both the political elite and the electorate. Within these interpretations, the role of parliamentary boroughs dominated by electoral patrons has been seen as an important feature. This article considers one such borough, Newton in Lancashire. Often presented as the archetypal 'pocket borough', Newton's parliamentary elections were indeed dominated by the lords of the manor, the Leghs of Lyme. The papers of this family show, however, that this electoral control was more complex than has previously been thought, and required significant electoral management by the family.

Keywords: political history; parliamentary elections; historic electoral organisations; Lancashire history

England's unreformed electoral system has long been a staple of eighteenth-century studies, but the study of parliamentary elections was given greater impetus by the publication in 1929 of Sir Lewis Namier's *The Structure of Politics at the Accession of George III*. Namier portrayed an electoral system where 'not one voter in twenty could freely exercise his statutory right'.[1] Electoral success was in large part dependent on corruption; the electorate was dominated by the landowning elite; and political issues played little role in determining election results.

With respect to the early eighteenth century, Namier's portrait of the electoral system was strongly rebutted by scholars such as Sir John Plumb, Bill Speck and Geoffrey Holmes, whose work demonstrated that in the context of that period's 'rage of party', there was a fierce contest to influence parliamentary elections, leading to a polarisation of electoral politics.[2] This created the opportunity for electoral participation, as rival candidates sought the support of the electorate. Consequently, relations between voters and those seeking their support were more complex and conditional than had previously been argued.

The Namierite model was also challenged in its stronghold of the later eighteenth century. John Phillips argued that the vast majority of the borough electorate was located in freeman and inhabitant boroughs that resisted electoral patronage;

that these were contested with increasing frequency in the late eighteenth and early nineteenth centuries; and that voters in these boroughs demonstrated a high level of electoral participation.[3] This was taken further in Frank O'Gorman's *Voters, Patrons, and Parties*, which argued that Namier's model concealed as much of the nature of the unreformed electoral system as it revealed.[4] Having accepted that electoral politics in the period was, to a large extent, dominated by elites, O'Gorman argued that such control was 'exercised conditionally amidst habits of widespread political involvement'.[5] By placing the actions of electoral patrons in the context of the deferential models of society advanced by historians such as Pocock, in which the distribution of patronage both imposed obligations on the recipient and demonstrated the obligations of the patron towards the local community,[6] O'Gorman moved beyond the simple characterisation of such patronage as little more than bribery and corruption and advanced a more nuanced interpretation of the relationship between patron and constituency than had held sway previously.[7]

This article considers the south Lancashire constituency of Newton, a small town within the parish of Winwick. Newton has been characterised as 'the pocket borough *par excellence*', controlled by a single family whose patronage allowed it to dictate its Members throughout the seventeenth and eighteenth centuries.[8] This characterisation is based on the reality of Newton's electoral outcomes throughout this period; however, there are periods where the sources for Newton elections allow us to examine electoral process as well as outcome. These sources demonstrate that maintaining electoral dominance at Newton was not a simple or straightforward process; rather, it was one that required regular and dutiful attention, and on occasion, broader political contexts could pose significant threats to the control of its patron.

The Foundations of the Legh Interest

First returning Members of Parliament in 1558, Newton had initially been within the orbit of the electoral influence of the Duchy of Lancaster. However, it quickly fell under the control of the Fleetwoods of Cowick, Staffordshire.[9] When the manor was sold to this family in 1594, the right to nominate Newton's Members was explicitly included in the sale.[10] It appears, however, that by the 1640s the Fleetwood interest had been superseded. The Leghs of nearby Lyme, Cheshire held extensive lands in Cheshire and South Lancashire.[11] By 1640, the Leghs had become the dominant force in Newton elections, so that when in 1660 the head of the family, Richard Legh, purchased the barony of Newton for £3,500 he was further securing an already powerful electoral interest.[12]

Richard Legh had succeeded his uncle to the family estates while still a minor in 1643. An ardent Royalist in the 1650s, Richard Legh was returned for Newton to the Cavalier Parliament and as party labels emerged he proved himself a staunch Tory – hostile to Dissent and Catholicism alike, and opposing the exclusion of the Duke of York from the succession. On his death in 1687, Richard Legh was succeeded by his eldest son Peter, who was elected for Newton in 1685 when just 15.

It was to be his only parliament.[13] Following the Glorious Revolution, Peter consistently refused to swear the oaths to the new regime, despite the suggestion at the beginning of 1708 that he stand for election in Cheshire.[14] He nevertheless continued to exercise the family interest at Newton, and to take an active role in Cheshire elections, until his death in 1744.[15] In all such elections, Legh invariably used his interest in favour of Tory candidates, and all but one of the Members returned for Newton between 1685 and 1744 can be positively identified as Tories.

As a manorial borough with no corporate structure, Newton's administrative bodies – the courts leet and baron – were held by authority of the lord of the manor. The steward who presided over these courts was nominated by, and held office at the pleasure of, the lord of Newton, such that the power of local government at Newton flowed from the Leghs. This position at the head of local society, with Newton's inhabitants owing suit after 1660 to the head of the Legh family, undoubtedly conferred a status on the family that aided their management of the borough's parliamentary elections. It also conveyed a tangible electoral benefit, as the steward also served as returning officer in parliamentary elections.[16] That contemporaries were well aware of this advantage was evident during the 1685 election, when a candidate standing against the nominees of Richard Legh wrote to the under-sheriff of Lancashire of his fear that the returning officer would not be 'indifferent as by Law he ought to be'.[17] This candidate was comfortably defeated at this election by those nominated by Richard Legh, but he subsequently petitioned the Commons, claiming that his election had been wrongly denied by the partiality of the steward and returning officer, who had been Richard Legh's younger brother Thomas.[18] The Leghs were clearly highly attuned to the electoral value of controlling the role of steward and thereby the returning officer, and sought to maximise this value to their electoral interest.

Of equal benefit to the Leghs' electoral interest at Newton was their position as the borough's dominant landowning family. The Leghs' purchase of the lordship of Newton was the culmination of a notable extension, starting in the early seventeenth century, of their landholdings in the borough.[19] The precise extent of the Legh's property in Newton is difficult to determine, as only one rental from the period concerned with here has been found. Prepared in the late 1720s, it lists 100 leases at Newton from Peter Legh, of which 81 were freeholds granted to approximately sixty individuals.[20] All but 11 of these leases were for three lives, while the 11 exceptions were for ninety years dependent upon three lives, a form of lease that limited the term should those named in it prove particularly long-lived. The format of this document suggests, however, that it may not include all leases of land at Newton, and it gives no information about the land owned in the borough by other individuals.

A comparison between the holdings of the Leghs and those of other landowners is possible, however, for the years shortly after Peter Legh's death. A 1749 survey of the Leghs' Lancashire lands records over 110 leases of land at Newton made to approximately ninety individuals, indicating a level of landownership comparable to that recorded in the late 1720s.[21] The following year, a list of 'other' freeholders at

Newton was prepared, and this survey noted that sixteen individuals – including two women – owned freehold land in Newton, and that these freeholders had thirty-seven tenants leasing these lands.[22] This demonstrates that the Leghs enjoyed a dominant position at Newton in terms of landownership. This landholding dominance was translated into political power via the borough's franchise, which was based on the possession of property in the borough.

The Role of the Franchise

Two different types of property-based borough franchises existed in the unreformed electoral system – burgage and freeholder – and historians have generally thought that Newton's franchise resided in the burgage holders. In 1807, one political commentator described a burgage, for the purpose of parliamentary elections, as being 'one undivided and indivisible tenement, neither created nor capable of being created within time of memory, which has immemorially given a right of voting; or an entire and indivisible tenement, holden of superior lord of a borough, by an immemorial, certain rent distinctly reserved, to which the right of voting is incident'.[23] Consequently, the vote was attached to individual, specific properties. The vote at Newton, however, rested with the freeholders.[24] The conduct of contested elections in 1685 and 1690 show that what was contested at this point was the definition of what constituted a freeholder; there was no argument as to whether this was the basis of the franchise. While these questions would not lead to as heated and prolonged a period of electoral contestation as was the case in the 'pocket' borough of Mitchell during this period, they nevertheless give a crucial insight into the mechanics of electoral control at Newton.[25]

In these contested elections, Thomas Brotherton, a member of a long-established local family, challenged the candidates backed by the Legh family.[26] Brotherton was defeated at the poll in 1685 and 1690, and on both occasions he petitioned the Commons against these reverses. Although no copy of his petitions survive, a summary of his claims in 1690 concerning the right to vote at Newton is contained in a letter to Peter Legh from one of his legal advisers. The key issue at stake was the definition of the franchise, and specifically the precise definition of a freeholder: Brotherton argued this should include all those who held land in the borough by freehold leases, and those who did so by leases determined solely in years. Legh was expected to argue 'that None but freeholders ought to vote'.[27] Brotherton's petitions were not heard by the Commons, and as no further petitions to the Commons referring to the nature of the franchise at Newton were made before 1797, it must be assumed that the definition put forward by the Leghs in 1690 held good until that time. Newton was a freeholder, rather than a burgage, borough. The vote was therefore attached to property, and as such the possession of land was crucial to the management of its elections.

The claim and counterclaim detailed in expectation of a hearing before the elections committee in 1690 reveals not only the nature of Newton's franchise, but also the way in which this franchise underpinned the Leghs' domination of the borough's elections.[28] As part of his preparations to defend Brotherton's claims, Peter Legh asked the staunch Tory Roger Kenyon, Clerk of the Peace for Lancashire and Member of Parliament for Clitheroe between 1690 and 1695, to examine Newton's previous election returns.[29] Kenyon investigated Brotherton's claim that the return of 1621 had been made in the name of the charterers and populace, and informed Legh that this return had instead been made in the name of the majority of the charterers (i.e., those who owned land in fee simple and who paid a 'chief rent' to the lord of the manor). This led Legh's uncle Thomas to express concern about the implications of this for the Legh interest, as it would exclude from the franchise Legh's tenants who held land under leases for lives.[30] Thomas wrote to his nephew of his fear that, should Kenyon's description of the 1621 return become public knowledge, it was possible that Newton tenants dependent upon the Leghs could be excluded from the borough's electorate. This would leave only the much smaller number of charterers, the borough's more substantial inhabitants who may have been able to resist the blandishments of the Leghs in order to 'chuse one or both Burgesses themselves'.[31] Thomas Legh feared that a much smaller electorate, composed only of charterers, would prove a greater temptation to other local notables with aspirations to secure control of a Commons seat: the smaller electorate would, by reducing the number of voters who would require treating, have made it easier for an aspiring patron to establish an interest in the borough.[32]

The concerns expressed by Thomas Legh clearly indicate the way in which the possession of land at Newton and the nature of the borough's franchise combined to provide a sure foundation for his nephew's electoral interest. The less substantial inhabitants of Newton, who may have been susceptible to the persuasions of rival candidates such as Brotherton, were to be excluded from voting. At the same time, the electorate was not to be so small as to make the prospects of challenging the Legh interest attractive to alternative patrons; or consist of only of the most substantial inhabitants, the charterers, who might at some point in the future cast off the Legh interest. Instead, the electorate was to consist of the borough's freeholders who, by dint of the Leghs' position as the dominant landowners in the borough, would form the basis of the Legh interest.

The Elections of the Early 1690s

This might suggest that once he had assumed control of the family interest in 1687, Peter Legh would be able to dispose of his electoral control as he saw fit, so that the sharpening of political divisions between Whig and Tory that took place after the Glorious Revolution – both at Westminster and in the political nation at large – would have little effect on Newton elections. The Legh papers demonstrate, however, that partisan considerations could place restrictions on the freedom with which Peter Legh exercised his proprietorial influence in the borough, most notably in the early 1690s when developments whose roots lay partly in partisan conflict led Peter Legh to fear a substantial challenge to his control of Newton.

The root of these developments was the conflict between Legh's non-juring Toryism and the zealous Whiggery of Charles, Lord Brandon, Lord Lieutenant of Lancashire from 1689 until his death in 1702. An ardent advocate in the early 1680s of the exclusion of the Duke of York from the succession, Brandon had been forced, following his conviction for complicity in the Rye House Plot, to cooperate with James II after 1685. Once freed from this obligation by the Glorious Revolution, however, Brandon returned to the Whig fold and in the following decade used his position as lord lieutenant to attack what he viewed as the unacceptable strength of Toryism in the county.[33] As part of this campaign, Brandon attempted to undermine the electoral interest of Lancashire's Tories in all but one of the county's six parliamentary boroughs, including Newton.[34]

The vehicle for Brandon's challenge at Newton was Thomas Brotherton. Brotherton's father had been a lukewarm Royalist during the civil wars, and Brotherton himself proved to be, like both Richard and Peter Legh, a zealous Tory.[35] Brotherton's candidacy in 1685 is probably best explained in terms of his personal ambition to enter the Commons. A belief that his family's standing in the borough justified such a pretension may also have played a part, as may irritation that Richard Legh had nominated a minor: his 15-year-old son Peter. Brotherton does not appear to have entered the lists at the 1689 election, but did so the following year in alliance with Sir James Forbes, against the candidates nominated by Peter Legh. In 1690, however, Brotherton's candidacy was clearly connected to broader political considerations as he allied himself with Lancashire's leading Whigs.

Nine days before the 1690 election, Thomas Legh reported that Brotherton was standing with the support of not only Brandon, but also two of Brandon's most prominent supporters in Lancashire politics: Thomas Norris and Roger Kirkby, both Whigs. Their aim was reported to be to 'take no [more] notice of ye present Lrd [of the manor] than of an inanimate creature', and thereby satisfy Brotherton's pretensions to a seat in the Commons and Brandon's desire to undermine Lancashire's Tory interest.[36] Brotherton and Forbes were overwhelmingly defeated, gaining only 20 and 19 votes respectively against the 47 cast for each of Legh's candidates, but Brotherton's vigorous canvassing and the support he received from Brandon rattled the Leghs.[37] Shortly before the election, George Cholmondeley, scion of Cheshire's leading family and one of the Legh candidates, wrote that Peter Legh's uncle and election agent, Thomas, had experienced 'some jealousies and mistrusts' among the local population, and that Peter Legh had needed to visit the borough, where he 'conferr'd & sounded his friends & tenants' to ensure that his interest was 'firm & right'.[38]

The need for such measures clearly demonstrates the concern that Brotherton and Brandon's challenge caused among the Legh interest. Rather than regard the success of his candidates as inevitable, Legh was acutely aware of the threat posed by the combination of Brotherton's local interest and Brandon's influence as lord lieutenant. Such concerns circumscribed Legh's freedom of choice when the death of the sitting Member, Sir John Chicheley, in March 1691 prompted a by-election. When John Bennet, a Cambridgeshire man whose brother was then serving as rector of Winwick, asked a mutual friend to approach Legh on his behalf, Bennet laid particular emphasis on his claim that 'one of my greatest designs is to oppose Mr Brotherton',[39] and a challenge from Brotherton was confidently forecast.[40] Brotherton did indeed begin to canvass, and it seems likely that he again drew support from Brandon for this endeavour.[41]

At the beginning of June, Peter Legh received a letter from the Earl of Derby, Lancashire's leading peer and a Tory,[42] recommending that he support Bennet's election 'for he has friends in the house of Commons & money too perhaps sufficient to cope with Brotherton'.[43] Legh accepted this recommendation, and Brotherton – who, in December 1691, finally withdrew from the Commons his petition against the 1690 election return – decided against contesting the by-election.[44] Support for Bennet's candidacy had been urged on Legh by figures of local prominence, and Legh's own uncle recommended throwing the Legh interest behind Bennet as something which 'yr best Friends in these parts mightily desire'.[45] The correspondence relating to this by-election suggests that Bennet was portrayed to Legh as the candidate most likely to defeat the challenge of Brotherton, and this in turn indicates that the threat posed by Brotherton was one not lightly dismissed by Legh. The pretensions of Brotherton to a seat at Newton were defeated in 1690 and 1691, but it is clear that Peter Legh was either unwilling or unable to dismiss such challenges (or perhaps both).

Brotherton drew support from those such as Brandon who, for partisan reasons, wished to attack Peter Legh's interest at Newton. The ways in which broader political issues could limit Legh's freedom of action at Newton cannot, however, be viewed purely in terms of contested elections. As a non-juror, Legh was the target of particular loathing from Brandon and other Whigs in positions of local authority. In the summer of 1691, for example, he was indicted at the Cheshire assizes for his refusal to take the oaths, but of far greater import was the allegations made against Legh in the Lancashire Plot three years later.[46] In the early 1690s, a small group of conspirators sought to implicate Lancashire and Cheshire Catholics in the conveying of lands to the use of the Catholic Church. Once the credibility of this evidence was undermined and a charge of perjury against the informers seemed likely, they claimed that several Catholics and two Anglicans had been involved in a conspiracy for a Jacobite rising in the north-west, an allegation that was pursued enthusiastically by the region's Whigs. One of the two Anglicans against whom such accusations were made was Peter Legh.[47] It was alleged that Peter Legh had, in 1689, received a commission to serve as a colonel of horse during a planned Jacobite rising, and that he had passed further commissions to other individuals. In July 1694, Legh's house at Lyme was searched and Legh was arrested. After a period of imprisonment in Chester Castle, Legh was subsequently kept under house arrest before being transported to the Tower of London, where he stayed for over a month before he was returned to Chester to stand trial.[48] During the summer of 1694, however, Roger Kenyon had been systematically gathering evidence to discredit the allegations, a process that was greatly aided by the decision of one of the original accusers to give evidence as to the false nature of the allegations. This former conspirator introduced two friends of Legh to the conspirators. Posing as potential accomplices, Legh's friends were admitted to several details of how the Lancashire Plot accusations were fabricated. The two friends of Legh were Legh Banks (a cousin of Peter Legh) and Edward Beresford. Their evidence further undermined the Lancashire Plot, leading to the collapse of the trials of the accused at Manchester and Chester in October 1694, and to Legh's release.[49]

Although he refused to take the oaths to William and Mary, Legh left no evidence of involvement in any of the Jacobite plots and conspiracies that undoubtedly occurred in Lancashire during the 1690s. Despite this, he had suffered a lengthy period of imprisonment and had had both his life and his estates placed in jeopardy by a group of professional liars. These memories combined with the obligations he had incurred to individuals who had assisted in his acquittal to influence strongly Legh's behaviour at the 1695 election. His debt to his cousin Legh Banks was obvious, and at the election Banks was returned for Newton to his one and only Parliament. The corollary of such gratitude was Legh's dissatisfaction with those who he felt had not provided aid at his time of need. This explains Legh's decision not to renew his support for George Cholmondeley. Cholmondeley wished to continue to represent Newton, but Lord Cholmondeley, George's elder brother, had not supported Legh openly and, despite George Cholmondeley himself having made representations to the King on Legh's behalf, Legh wrote to Lord Cholmondeley that the need to 'gratify some Gentlemen (wth. my interest at Newton) yt was instrumental in delivering me' from the Lancashire Plot accusations meant that he was unable to return his brother.[50]

The beneficiary of this decision was Thomas Brotherton. Since the 1691 by-election, Brotherton had forsaken his dalliance with the Whig interest and instead allied himself with Lancashire's Tories, being elected on this interest at the Liverpool by-election of 1694 and assisting in a legal capacity those accused in the Lancashire Plot.[51] In October 1695, Brotherton lobbied Legh for his nomination to Newton, emphasising his split from Brandon (who was, by this point, earl of Macclesfield), his activities during the Lancashire Plot trials, and his readiness to be 'serviceable' to Legh.[52] Following recent experiences, Legh would have been keenly aware of the need for such assistance if he were to be accused again of treasonable activity, and if not he was surely reminded of it by his friends.[53] Consequently, Legh supported Brotherton's return at Newton in 1695, so that both Newton Members returned in 1695 owed their election in large part to their roles in defending the Lancashire Plot accusations.

It may be that Brotherton's election was, at least in part, due to another factor too. This is suggested by the way in which Peter Legh dealt with the request of Roger Kenyon for a seat at Newton. Kenyon had been unstinting in his efforts to expose the Lancashire Plot allegations as fabrications, and had therefore contributed greatly to Legh's eventual acquittal. After Kenyon had withdrawn from the Clitheroe election of 1695, it was thought likely that Legh would offer him a seat at Newton, and in October 1695 Kenyon made an application on his own behalf and that of Legh's uncle, Sir John Ardern. Despite his gratitude for Kenyon's assistance during 1694, however, Legh denied the request, citing his 'unfortunate circumstances'.[54] The obvious question is why Kenyon's greater efforts to undermine the Lancashire Plot allegations yielded less gratitude at the 1695 election than Brotherton's lesser activity had. The simple answer would be that Kenyon had left his application too late, and that Legh was already engaged to Banks and Brotherton; however, Brotherton's letters to Legh date from just a week before Kenyon made his request. Another plausible explanation is that Legh feared that, if rejected, Brotherton might mount an electoral challenge at Newton, and that Legh wished to avoid a contested election at Newton.

The hypothesis that Legh's decision to support Brotherton stemmed partly from a desire to prevent a contest is neither confirmed nor contradicted by the surviving evidence. What is undeniable is that in 1695, Peter Legh's freedom of action at Newton had been severely limited by the events of the previous two years. This much is indicated by the fact that, in addition to refusing the applications of Ardern, Cholmondeley and Kenyon, Legh refused a further two such requests citing obligations to other 'friends'.[55] Circumstances arising from the political conflict in Lancashire, reflecting national political divisions between Tory and Whig, had therefore determined for Peter Legh the individuals who were to be returned at Newton in 1695, removing the freedom of choice that would be expected from a dominant proprietor in a borough such as Newton.

The constraints placed upon Legh at the 1695 election could be viewed as unique, and indeed there is no record that Legh was ever involved in another episode as serious as that of 1694. However, Legh could not be as assured of this as it is tempting for modern observers to be. In 1696, for example, he was arrested in the aftermath of the failed Assassination Plot, and following the discovery in 1722 of the Atterbury Plot, Legh felt it prudent to write to the Secretary of State of his 'intentions to live easily under the Government', and to assure the Secretary that he would soon arrive in London as directed.[56] In the years immediately following the Glorious Revolution, Legh's activity as patron of Newton was affected by the divisions, in both national and Lancashire politics, between Whig and Tory. Such divisions had occasioned a challenge to Legh's interest in 1690 and 1691, a challenge which, though unsuccessful, had caused Legh a significant degree of concern. Four years later, his freedom of action as the borough's proprietor had been severely limited by the aftermath of a local, party cause that reflected divisions in the national body politic concerning the question of allegiance to the Williamite regime. Even a borough such as Newton was not immune to the effects of the 'rage of party', and even an interest as strong as Legh's at Newton was not invulnerable to potential electoral threats.

The Role of Party and the Newton Electorate

The events of the early 1690s demonstrate that the division of the political nation along Whig–Tory lines affected Newton elections at the level of the borough's political elite. They do not, however, reveal whether the electors and inhabitants of

Newton regarded elections in such terms. Peter Legh's papers do offer some insight into this question, though.

At the 1708 general election, John Ward and Peter Legh's brother Thomas both stood for re-election at Newton, and – as they had been in 1705 – were returned unchallenged. An account of the election sent to Ward reveals, however, that the election did not pass with complete ease. Ward was informed that, in the absence of the candidates from the court of election, it was only the presence of a number of substantial charterers that prevented 'a very scandalous appearance' at the election.[57] The concern for the conduct of, and attendance at, the election is clear, and the contents of the manorial steward's speech to those assembled at the election is revealing:

> we are to proceed to the Election of two Burgesses to represent this Burrough for ye Ensuing Parliament I can say without Flattery you have been more Unanimous and discreet in yr Elections for many years than any Burrough or Corporn. in ye County. And the Reason of this is plain, You are all Members of ye Church of Engld there are no Schisms nor Factions amongst you, nor do any base or mean Principles prevail amongst you … As to ye Gentlemen who servd you in the last Parliament and who offer themselves ag[ain] to serve you in this, all I shall say is that they servd you faithfully & ingeniously. They are well affected to ye Q and Govermt. They are neither Soldiers nor Pentioners and theref. fitter to be trusted with our Church & Estates. In One word they are after our own Hearts and therf (if you pleas) let Us now proceed to Elect and Return them.[58]

The patron's nominees were presented to the borough's voters, and probably to its inhabitants as well, for their approval. This was requested rather than demanded, and obtaining the assent of the local community was therefore central to the election ritual at Newton, implying some type of contract between the Members being returned and those in whose name they were returned. Further, the partisan overtones of the steward's speech to the electoral court are undeniable. The lack of political division at Newton was attributed to the loyalty of its inhabitants to the established Church, and the candidates' suitability to serve was proclaimed with reference to their loyalty to Church and State and their freedom from Court influence.

Further evidence of the importance of party to the Newton electorate is largely limited to the constituency's addresses to the Crown on contemporary political issues. During Queen Anne's reign, for example, Newton addressed the Crown on at least three occasions: the victory at Ramillies in 1706, the peace negotiations of 1712, and the conclusion of the Treaty of Utrecht the following year.[59] Addresses from parliamentary boroughs on such occasions had become routine, and caution should be taken when examining such documents. The 1712 and 1713 addresses are strikingly Tory in tone, but it is difficult to discern whether this was a reflection of the political opinions of those in whose name the addresses were presented (the steward, bailiff, burgesses and inhabitants of Newton), or whether such sentiments stemmed from the Toryism of Peter Legh and the borough's Members.

Such difficulties also exist when examining an address prepared by twenty-two of Newton's inhabitants for presentation to the borough's Members in 1704. This expressed thanks for the Members' assistance in the swift passage of supply (funding for government approved by Parliament) and condemned the Scottish Act of Security, before moving on to thank them for their role in defending the rights of the Commons in their dispute with the Lords over the Aylesbury election case.[60] The author(s) of the address were clearly well informed about political developments, but the address went further. It also demonstrated Tory sympathies by expressing gratitude to Newton's Members for their support of 'that Excellent bill brought in to prevent that Scandalous Practice of Occasional Conformity'.[61] The signatories of this address requested that the borough's steward communicate it to their Members, but it is unclear if it was initiated by these inhabitants or by a representative of Peter Legh. The manuscript address is intriguingly endorsed 'not thought proper to be sent'.[62] This may suggest that the address was started in Newton without Legh's knowledge, but it is also possible that it was initiated and halted by Legh or one of his agents.

Aside from these addresses and the single election speech, little other evidence survives relating to the national political consciousness of Newton's inhabitants. The borough's Members were expected to forward copies of London newspapers to Newton, suggesting a desire on the part of the borough's inhabitants to remain informed of national developments,[63] but such evidence of an awareness at Newton of national political developments, and of the importance of such national issues to the borough's electorate and inhabitants, is far from conclusive. The stridently Tory sentiments evident in the borough's addresses and the one surviving election speech may be thought to demonstrate that the borough's political elite, its patron, his electoral managers and Newton's Members viewed elections from a partisan perspective, such that partisan, ideological sentiments became an important part of the election process at Newton in the First Age of Party. It cannot, however, be determined to what extent inhabitants of Newton shared, opposed, or had any view at all on Peter Legh's Tory beliefs.

Maintaining the Legh Interest

Though the evidence of the political opinions of Newton's voters and population is scarce, it is clear that Peter Legh was not content to rely solely on his position as the borough's dominant landowner to ensure electoral control. Legh, his election managers and Newton's Members also carried out many of the rituals of interest-making and maintenance that characterised the unreformed electoral system.[64] Evidence of electoral treating survives for the 1685, 1690 and 1691 elections, for example. In 1685, it was reported that Thomas Brotherton had 'designe[d] to create his interest solely in the mobile fermen=ting [fomenting] them for -3- weeks or a month before the Elec[ti]on, wth. drinke', and although in response the Leghs had spent only £42 1s 6d on treating at this election, by the 1691 by-election the cost of managing the Legh interest had trebled to £129 11s 1d.[65]

Treating also took place at uncontested elections, demonstrated by the surviving bills for expenses at the 1722, 1734 and 1741 elections. On these occasions, over £100 was spent on entertaining Newton's inhabitants in numerous public houses, and it seems likely that the lack of evidence for treating at elections between 1691 and 1722 is due to the accidental survival of sources rather than the absence of treating. That this became the norm at Newton is suggested by the accounts of the expenditure of Legh's nephew and heir at the 1747, 1754, 1761 and 1768 elections, accounts which also reveal that the election ritual in the borough extended to providing music for those attending the court of election, chairing the successful candidates, and ringing the bells of Newton's chapel.[66] A letter written to Peter Legh's estate steward in 1741 clearly demonstrates that such treating had come to be expected, as the steward was informed that 'no side is pleased with the Newton election ... the people murmer, complain they had not drink enough, and are more displeased with this Election than any they ever had'.[67]

Treating was not confined to elections. In 1713, John Ward – Newton's Member since 1703 – offered to send money to Newton to allow an appropriate celebration of the Treaty of Utrecht.[68] Members frequently financed races at Newton too; in 1720, Peter Legh informed the sitting Member Sir Francis Leicester that, following his sponsorship of just such an event, 'yr health was kindly remember'd', since 'yr Race ... brought so much Company [to Newton] they were drank dry & I found one House inlarging the sellars'.[69] As with treating at elections, such events soon came to be expected. This much is clear from a letter written to Legh in 1727, which stated that 'tis taken very ill by many in the Town yt have brewed great Quantities of Ale that there is no money sent for a race as usual'.[70] Maintaining interest with the inhabitants of Newton was not limited to such treating. Newton Members were not spared such mundane duties as sending copies of national newspapers to the borough, and it is again evident that the failure to carry out this duty could lead to censure from the local community: in 1714, the complaints of local inhabitants were relayed to one of Newton's Members about his neglect in dispatching papers to the borough.[71]

It could be objected that the Leghs' efforts to maintain their interest merely masked the true nature of proprietorial dominance. Contemporaries were confident in the control that Legh exercised over the borough: when asking for Legh's nomination to Newton in 1714, the Jacobite Tory William Shippen observed that Legh had 'preserved it [Newton] easie under all disadvantages for above 25 years & I doubt not will maintain it forever'.[72] That such views were not uncommon is clear from the way in which Newton came to be seen as a Tory port at times of electoral storm. In 1699, for example, rumours of an imminent dissolution led Edward Brereton, a Tory then sitting for Denbigh boroughs who feared defeat at the next election, to write requesting Legh's nomination. Three years later, the leading Tory backbencher John Grobham Howe was returned for Newton due to fears that stiff Whig opposition would lead to his defeat in Gloucestershire.[73] Common to all such requests from Tories who feared electoral defeat elsewhere was the belief that Legh's control was absolute.

At times, however, Legh himself was less certain of this. He does not appear to have doubted that, in the words of one observer writing in 1701, his family's interest at Newton was 'sufficient to influence an election according to their own minds'.[74] Legh was, however, less certain than many contemporaries that this would continue indefinitely without careful tending of his interest. Rumours of the death of one of Newton's sitting Members in February 1701 led to Legh being asked to return the Tory Thomas Coke at the anticipated by-election. Legh agreed, but requested that 'If this affair comes to an election, I desire that we may have Mr Cook's company at that time. To prevent some sort of censure that formerly has been made – that Newton Members seldom was [sic] known to the voters.'[75] The rumours of the sitting Member's death proved to be inaccurate, Coke never sat for Newton, and Legh's comments could be seen as nothing more than a wish to prevent slurs on himself and his borough. They do, however, reveal a concern to satisfy a desire by Newton's inhabitants to have their Members attend borough elections. Such a motive may not have sprung from a fear that Legh would not be able to secure Coke's return if he did not attend the election, but could imply that Legh was concerned that such failures to satisfy local sentiments, if they became frequent, could erode the basis of his interest.

That Legh was sensitive to the long-term health of his interest, and that there were boundaries in his relationship with the Newton electorate that he would be wise not to overstep, was evident in 1713. At this election, Legh nominated Abraham Blackmore to take the seat previously held by Legh's brother Thomas – a vacancy forced by a combination of the requirement of the Landed Qualification Act of 1711 that all Members for borough seats possess a landed estate worth £300 per annum, and the economic straits of Thomas Legh.[76] Lord Treasurer Oxford had agreed to provide Thomas Legh with a sinecure, in return for which Peter Legh would allow Oxford to name Thomas's successor at Newton. Oxford settled on Blackmore, who was duly returned. Legh found, however, that such manoeuvres prompted 'unexpected grumbles' at Newton, and six months after his election, Blackmore wrote of his concern that 'reflections' were being cast in the borough on Legh's behaviour and that 'contested elections' were being mentioned as a possible consequence.[77] These disturbances could, perhaps, have had a partisan aspect, as Blackmore conjectured that such sentiments may have been related to Tory divisions between the party's Jacobite and Hanoverian wings. Leading figures in this latter group were the Finches, most notably Daniel, Earl of Nottingham and Heneage, Lord Guernsey, while Blackmore was closely aligned with the Jacobite-leaning faction.[78] In March 1714 Blackmore wrote that, in his opinion, the rumblings of discontent at Newton were being encouraged by a man who had 'listed himself under the Finches banner',[79] and this may perhaps owe something to Nottingham's brother Henry Finch at this point being Rector of Winwick (the parish in which Newton lay).[80]

It also seems likely that the individual to whom Blackmore was referring was an individual described in 1715 as a 'man in town [Newton] that was a Lancashire man but had lived some time in London'.[81] If this was the case, then it is possible that

Blackmore's assessment was correct. A Newton inhabitant recently returned from London, who brought with him both political news and opinions relating to current developments at Westminster, had begun to criticise Peter Legh in terms relating to the current divisions among Tories and might even, potentially, draw on the support of the Rector of Winwick. Such an interpretation is plausible, but the uneasiness at Newton noted between 1713 and 1715 should also be seen in the context of the relationship between the borough's patron and electorate. In February 1715, reports reached Legh that an unnamed man had been creating interest against Legh's candidates. The attempt was dismissed as a 'foolish fancy' and indeed there is no evidence that a sustained challenge was mounted to the Legh candidates at this election.[82] That such an attempt should be contemplated, however, suggests that there were individuals at Newton who, though few in number, were unhappy with Legh's imposition of Blackmore in 1713. Whether this was for reasons of national politics, or a concern not to be taken for granted by the lord of Newton, this unhappiness was sufficiently strong for them to contemplate supporting a candidate or candidates opposed to the nominees of the lord of the manor at the next election.

Consequently, the concern Legh expressed in 1701 not to ride rough-shod over Newton's inhabitants in nominating the borough's Members could well have indicated a necessary sensitivity to local mood rather than a mere concern for electoral decorum. It is, for example, notable that of the fourteen men who sat for Newton between 1685 and 1744, only Howe and Blackmore had no connection with the borough and its region. All the others, save two, were members of the Lancashire and Cheshire gentry. The two remaining men were Sir John Chicheley and John Bennet, both of whom were from Cambridgeshire families. Chicheley had, however, married into the Leghs; and at the time of Bennet's election his brother was serving as rector of Winwick.[83] It therefore seems that Newton served as a means by which members of the north-west elite could enter the Commons, a fact that reflects the circles in which Peter Legh moved. It may also indicate an unwillingness to impose outsiders on the borough, an unwillingness that was probably rooted, at least in part, in a certain hostility among Newton's voters and inhabitants to candidates with no local connections or ties.

A recognition that his position as proprietor of Newton's parliamentary seats required careful maintenance of his standing in the borough is clearly implied by Legh's alertness to opportunities to bolster his electoral interest, and his sensitivity to developments that may have undermined it. Both of these qualities can be observed in his actions between 1720 and 1735 concerning the right to nominate the curate of Newton. Rather than being a parish in its own right, Newton possessed a dependent chapelry (and Richard Legh had financed the building of a new chapel in the mid-1680s) within the parish of Winwick.[84] Consequently, Newton was served by a curate. From 1686 until 1731, this post was occupied by Edward Allanson, who in 1727 wrote to Peter Legh of how he had 'promised Yr Good Father that I woud do my endeavour to preserve the Peace of the Burrough and be myself firm attach'd to ye Interest of yr Family here, and you must know, yt I have religiously and strictly observ'd this my promise and will do it to [the] End of yt short Life yt remains to me'.⁸⁵ Allanson's services to the Legh interest certainly extended to assisting Peter Legh to preserve the family's domination of Newton elections. He acted as an intermediary between Legh and aspirants to a seat at Newton, actively participated in courts of election, and was recognised by Newton Members to have both the ear of Peter Legh and an acute perception of the mood of the borough.⁸⁶ The important role played by Allanson is also indicated by the lack of any evidence in this period (save the possibly single exception cited here) that the Rector of Winwick actively engaged in Newton elections.

Legh's appreciation of Allanson's role became clear when the curate fell seriously ill in 1720, and Legh realised that the right to nominate Allanson's successor might rest not in his hands, but in those of the Rector of Winwick. Steps were taken to investigate whether a document dating from 1687 had transferred this right of nomination to the Leghs in return for their financing the rebuilding of the chapel, but Legh's inquiries received discouraging replies from the diocesan hierarchy. Allanson's recovery eased Legh's worries, but the extent of Legh's concern to control the nomination to the curacy of Newton became apparent in 1723 when rumours circulated that the advowson of Winwick would soon be offered for sale.⁸⁷ Buying this advowson would have secured Legh's right to nominate Newton's curate, and he was keen to pursue such a purchase, confiding that though the purchase 'will be all dead Money ... I have a little Piety & a great deal of Politicks for so doing'.⁸⁸

Thus, the importance of having a local clergyman to act as a reliable agent of the Legh interest was made clear, and Peter Legh's own awareness of the need for constant vigilance in maintaining his interest at Newton was demonstrated. The extent of Legh's commitment to preserving the political influence he derived from the right to nominate Newton's curate became clear following Allanson's death in 1731, after which Legh engaged in a legal dispute with the rector and patron of Winwick over the right of nomination. The final settlement of this dispute in 1735 largely preserved Legh's right, and the considerable effort and expense that he went to in defending his claim indicates both the importance he attached to the influence of Newton's curate, and his determination to oppose developments which could undermine his electoral interest at Newton.

Conclusion

Legh's efforts throughout his life to maintain and bolster his electoral interest at Newton confirm O'Gorman's model of electoral patrons needing to lavish time, attention and money on the constituencies in which they aspired to exercise an interest. A large part of *Voters, Patrons and Parties* is given over to establishing a typology of English and Welsh parliamentary boroughs, in which emphasis is placed on 'the basic elements of control ... which determine the character of electoral relationships in a group of constituencies'; this complements the more traditional categorisation of boroughs, established by the Porritts, according to franchise type.⁸⁹ Newton is included among the second of O'Gorman's five categories, that of proprietorial boroughs 'in which the vote was treated as a form of property and the voting process as a transaction in property relationships'.[90] According to O'Gorman, the electoral control of proprietorial boroughs depended 'overwhelmingly upon the possession of property', such that 'elections were determined ... by property transactions rather than by political conflicts'.[91] Consequently, the role accorded to 'the usual rituals of canvassing, treating and speeches' in establishing proprietorial control in such boroughs was strictly secondary to considerations of property and legal propriety.[92] Although O'Gorman does note that 'in some of these boroughs the patrons appear to have gone much further in order to protect their investment',[93] he portrays such actions as an attempt to prevent electors 'providing awkward testimony in the event of a petition', rather than making any meaningful contribution in and of themselves to the maintenance of electoral control.[94]

Such a description does not do justice to Peter Legh's activities as patron of Newton. For O'Gorman, control of proprietorial boroughs depended overwhelmingly on the possession of property with other forms of interest-making and maintaining relegated to a very minor role, while this article has argued that at Newton, Peter Legh's status as lord of the manor and dominant property owner, and his concern to maintain a good relationship with Newton's inhabitants, were both essential to securing his electoral control. The means of establishing such control in the proprietorial borough of Newton seem remarkably similar to those O'Gorman identified as being essential to maintaining an interest in what he describes as the patronage boroughs: that is, 'settled, natural interests ... based ... on the solid foundations of landed property, services to the constituency, and the goodwill of the electors'.[95]

Peter Legh's formative experience in Newton politics had been dealing with challenges to his family's interest. His apprenticeship as an electoral proprietor had demonstrated how a discontented local notable could contest parliamentary elections by creating an interest through treating the 'mobile'; that some elements of this group were susceptible to such blandishments; and that in such circumstances care had to be taken to preserve the loyalty of Newton voters to the Legh interest. It had also become apparent to Legh that Newton elections could not be isolated from political developments in the county as a whole – developments which bore close relation to the nature of political conflict on the national stage – and that his political enemies would gladly accept any opportunity that presented itself to attack both Legh and his interest at Newton. Given such experiences it is scarcely surprising that, rather than relying solely on his influence as lord of the manor of Newton and the borough's dominant landowner, Legh sought to preserve and bolster his interest with Newton's voters and inhabitants.

On his death in 1744, Legh was succeeded by his nephew and namesake, whose papers are, unfortunately, far less interesting to political historians than those of his uncle. The evidence that does survive concerning Newton elections after 1744 indicates, however, that many of the features identified here as characterising the borough's elections between 1685 and 1744 remained. Treating bills for elections demonstrate that Peter Legh the younger remained concerned to satisfy local expectations in this regard, and in 1768, one of Newton's charterers made preparations to challenge Legh's nominees, a pretension which, although not apparently carried to a poll had obvious parallels with the earlier interventions of Thomas Brotherton.[96] In consequence it would seem that Peter Legh's concerns as proprietor of Newton were shared by an heir who had not experienced the types of problems with which Legh himself had had to deal in the 1690s.

Legh's conduct shows that electoral control at Newton rested on both a dominant position in respect of landownership, and a willingness to undertake the paternalistic duties O'Gorman identified as central to maintaining an electoral interest in what he described as patronage boroughs. Newton may well have been 'the pocket borough *par excellence*', but that it remained so was due to the considerable efforts of Peter Legh.[97]

Acknowledgements

This article draws on, expands and furthers my research that underpinned the constituency of article on Newton, of which I was co-author, in E. Cruickshanks, D. W. Hayton and S. Handley (eds), *The History of Parliament: The House of Commons, 1690–1715*, 2 (Cambridge: Cambridge University Press, 2002), pp. 332–6.

Notes

1. L. B. Namier, *The Structure of Politics at the Accession of George III* (London: Macmillan, rev. edn, 1957), p. 87.
2. J. H. Plumb, *The Growth of Political Stability in England 1675–1725* (London: Macmillan, 1967); J. H. Plumb, 'The Growth of the Electorate in England from 1600–1715', *Past and Present*, 45 (1969), 90–116; W. A. Speck, *Tory and Whig: The Struggle in the Constituencies 1701–1715* (London: Macmillan, 1970); G. S. Holmes, *The Electorate and the National Will in the First Age of Party* (Kendal: University of Lancaster, 1976).
3. J. A. Phillips, 'The Structure of Electoral Politics in Unreformed England', *Journal of British Studies*, 45 (1979/80), 76–100; J. A. Phillips, 'Popular Politics in Unreformed England', *Journal of Modern History*, 52 (1980), 599–625; J. A. Phillips, *Electoral Behaviour in Unreformed England: Plumpers, Splitters and Straights* (Princeton: Princeton University Press, 1982). Phillips's argument, that the higher frequency of elections in constituencies with larger electorates demonstrates a more participatory electoral system than was previously thought, has been emphasised by the comprehensive work undertaken by the Eighteenth Century Political Participation and Electoral Culture project (https://ecppec.ncl.ac.uk/ [accessed 22 February 2024]). See, for example, the comments in M. O. Grenby and E. Chalus, 'Elections in Eighteenth Century England: Polling, Politics and Participation', *Parliamentary History*, 43 (2024), 5–19.
4. F. O'Gorman, *Voters, Patrons and Parties: The Unreformed Electorate of Hanoverian England, 1734–1832* (Oxford: Clarendon Press, 1989).
5. *Ibid.*, p. 7.

6 J. G. A. Pocock, 'The Classical Theory of Deference', *American Historical Review*, 71 (1976), 516–23.
7 O'Gorman, *Voters, Patrons and Parties*, pp. 225–44. For the practice of treating in the context of the contemporary legal position on electoral bribery and corruption, see M. Knights, *Trust and Distrust: Corruption in Office in Britain and its Empire, 1600–1850* (Oxford: Oxford University Press, 2021), pp. 99–101, 281–92.
8 Speck, *Tory and Whig*, p. 57.
9 P. W. Hasler (ed.), *The History of Parliament: The House of Commons, 1558–1603*, 1 (London: Her Majesty's Stationery Office, 1981), p. 190; W. Farrer and J. Brownbill (eds), *Victoria County History of the County of Lancaster*, 1 (London: Constable, 1906), pp. 374–5; A. Thrush and J. P. Ferris (eds), *The History of Parliament: The House of Commons, 1604–29*, 2 (Cambridge: Cambridge University Press, 2010), pp. 214–5.
10 E. and A. G. Porritt, *The Unreformed House of Commons*, 1 (Cambridge: Cambridge University Press, 1909) p. 97.
11 B. D. Henning (ed.), *The History of Parliament: The House of Commons, 1660–90*, 2 (London: Secker & Warburg, 1983), pp. 727–9.
12 S. K. Roberts (ed.), *The History of Parliament: The House of Commons, 1640–60*, 2 (Cambridge: Cambridge University Press, 2023), pp. 296–8.
13 W. Farrer and J. Brownbill (eds), *Victoria County History of the County of Lancashire*, 3 (London: Constable, 1907), p. 134; Henning, *House of Commons, 1660–90*, 2, pp. 728–9; Manchester, John Rylands Library (hereafter JRL), Legh MSS, muniments box A, indenture 27 October 1660; *ibid.*, deed of covenant, 31 October 1660.
14 JRL, Legh MSS, corresp., Thomas to Peter Legh, 24 January 1708.
15 P. J. Challinor, 'The Structure of Politics in Cheshire, 1660–1715' (PhD thesis, University of Wolverhampton, 1983); S. W. Baskerville, 'The Management of the Tory Interest in Lancashire and Cheshire, 1714–1747' (DPhil thesis, University of Oxford, 1976).
16 Oxford, Bodleian Library, MS Willis 46, fols 361, 420; Oxford, Bodleian Library, MS Willis 51, fols 69, 76.
17 JRL, Legh MSS, muniments box Z, Brotherton to under-sheriff of Lancashire, 22 April 1685.
18 *Ibid.*, poll book, 23 April 1685'; *ibid.*, petition of Brotherton, n.d. c.1685; *Journal of the House of Commons*, 9 (London: His Majesty's Stationery Office, 1802) p. 718. Henning (*House of Commons*, 1, p. 291) is mistaken in conjecturing that Brotherton petitioned solely against Peter Legh citing Legh's minority.
19 F. Gastrell, *Notitia Cestrienses, or Historical Notice of the Diocese of Chester*, ed. F. R. Raines (Manchester: Chetham Society, 1st series, 21), p. 264; Farrer and Brownbill, *Victoria County History*, 3, p. 134.
20 JRL, Legh MSS, muniments, box P, 'Newton register', n.d.
21 JRL, Legh MSS, muniments, box O, 'Lancashire Land Survey 1749', fols 18–35.
22 JRL, Legh MSS, muniments, box P, 'Newton freeholders 1750'.
23 R. Beatson, *A Chronological Register of Both House of the British Parliament*, 3 (London: Longman, Hurst, Rees and Orme, 1807), p. 202.

24 The following all refer to Newton as a burgage borough: Henning (*House of Commons*, 1, p. 291; R. R. Sedgwick (ed.), *The History of Parliament: The House of Commons, 1715–54*, 1 (London: Her Majesty's Stationery Office, 1970), p. 272; Speck, *Tory and Whig*, p. 70. L. B. Namier and J. H. Brooke (eds), *The History of Parliament: The House of Commons, 1754–1790*, 1 (London: Her Majesty's Stationery Office, 1964), p. 318 mistakenly claims that Newton's franchise lay in members of the corporation. Porritt, *Unreformed House of Commons*, 1, p. 97 describes Newton as a freeholder borough. O'Gorman, *Voters, Patrons and Parties*, p. 33 classes Newton as a burgage borough, but notes that the nature of the franchise was somewhat uncertain. Its nature as a freeholder borough was established in Cruickshanks, Hayton and Handley, *House of Commons*, 2, pp. 333–5.

25 J. Harris, 'Partnership and Popular Politics in a Cornish "Pocket" Borough, 1660–1714', *Parliamentary History*, 37 (2018), 350–68.

26 For these two elections, see Cruickshanks, Hayton and Handley, *House of Commons*, 2, pp. 333–5.

27 JRL, Legh MSS, muniments box Z, Roger Kenyon to Peter Legh, 16 March 1690; *ibid.*, account of Newton election, 1685; *ibid.*, 'a copy of those Mr Brotherton calls voters', n.d. *c.*1690; *ibid.*, counter-petition, n.d. *c.*1690; *ibid.*, corresp., Thomas to Peter Legh, n.d. *c.*1690.

28 Speck, *Tory and Whig*, pp. 47–8; Phillips, *Electoral Behaviour*, pp. 61–3: O'Gorman, *Voters, Patrons and Parties*, pp. 31–8.

29 JRL, Legh MSS, muniments box Z, Kenyon to Legh, 16 March 1690.

30 *Ibid.*, corresp., Thomas Legh to Peter Legh, n.d. *c.*1690. For Thomas Legh, see Henning, *House of Commons*, 2, p. 729.

31 JRL, Legh MSS, corresp., Thomas Legh to Peter Legh, n.d. *c.*1690.

32 *Ibid.*

33 L. K. J. Glassey, 'The Origins of Political Parties in Seventeenth Century Lancashire', *Transactions of the Historic Society of Lancashire and Cheshire*, 136 (1987), 45–7; Henning, *House of Commons*, 2, pp. 386–8.

34 S. N. Handley, 'Lancashire *c.*1689–*c.*1731: Some Aspects of the Interaction of Local and Central Affairs in an English County' (PhD thesis, University of Lancaster, 1989), pp. 314–20.

35 Farrer and Brownbill, *Victoria County History*, 3, pp. 134–5; Cruickshanks, Hayton and Handley, *House of Commons*, 3, pp. 360–3.

36 Preston, Lancashire Archives, Kenyon MSS, DDKe/9/63/7, Thomas Legh to Roger Kenyon, 2 March 1690.

37 JRL, Legh MSS, corresp., George Cholmondeley to Ld. Hugh Cholmondeley (*c.*March 1690).

38 *Ibid.*

39 National Library of Wales, Chirk Castle MSS E1073, John Bennet to Sir Richard Myddelton, 21 May 1691.

40 JRL, Legh MSS, corresp., Thomas Legh to Peter Legh, 21 May 1691.

41 *Ibid.*, Peter Legh to [?], 2 June 1691.

42 B. Coward, 'The Social and Political Position of the Earls of Derby in Later Seventeenth Century Lancashire', *Transactions of the Historic Society of Lancashire and Cheshire*, 132 (1982), 127–54.

43 JRL, Legh MSS, Earl of Derby to Peter Legh, 2 June 1691.

44 *Journal of the House of Commons*, 10 (London: His Majesty's Stationery Office, 1802) pp. 354–5, 428, 540, 570.

45 JRL, Legh MSS, corresp., Thomas Legh to Peter Legh, 21 May 1691.

46 *Ibid.*, Thomas Legh to Peter Legh, 26 July 1691; *ibid.*, Lettice Banks to Peter Legh, 6 October 1691.

47 E. L. Lonsdale, 'John Lunt and the Lancashire Plot 1694', *Transactions of the Historic Society of Lancashire and Cheshire*, 115 (1963), 91–106; P. A. Hopkins, 'The Commission for Superstitious Lands in the 1690s', *Recusant History*, 15 (1979–80), 263–82; R. Weil, *A Plague of Informers: Conspiracy and Political Trust in William III's England* (New Haven, CT: Yale University Press, 2012), pp. 217–47.

48 *Historical Manuscripts Commission, Fourteenth Report, Appendix, Part IV The Manuscripts of Lord Kenyon* (London: Her Majesty's Stationery Office, 1894), pp. 344–51, 363–6; *Calendar of State Papers Domestic, 1694–95*, pp. 308, 315, 316, 322.

49 *HMC Kenyon*, pp. 366–7, 387–94; Chester, Cheshire Archives, Shakerley MSS, 'a breife account of the severall persons & their evidences', n.d. *c*.1694; J. Addy, J. Harrop and P. McNiven (eds), *The Diary of Henry Prescott, Ll.B., Deputy Registrar of Chester Diocese* (Record Society of Lancashire and Cheshire, 133), pp. 898–9. For the Commons' investigation of the plot and the trials see London, British Library, Add. MS 46527, fol. 22; Oxford, Bodleian Library, MS Eng. hist. C.289, fol. 197; *ibid.*, MS Carte 130, fol. 353; *HMC Kenyon*, pp. 322–54. The Commons resolved that 'upon the informations and examinations before this House, it does appear, that there was a dangerous plot carried on against the King and government'; *Journal of the House of Commons*, 9, pp. 223–4.

50 JRL, Legh MSS, corresp., Peter Legh to Ld. Cholmondeley, n.d. *c*.1695; *ibid.*, Thomas Bankes to Peter Legh, n.d. *c*.1695 and 8 June 1695.

51 Preston, Lancashire Archives, Kenyon MSS DDKe/9/67/37, Thomas Marsden to Roger Kenyon, 27 March 1694; *HMC Kenyon*, pp. 284, 320–1; JRL, Legh MSS, corresp., Thomas Brotherton to [Edward Allanson], 12 October 1695; London, British Library, Egerton MS 720, fols 79–80.

52 JRL, Legh MSS, corresp., Brotherton to Peter Legh, 10 October [1695]; *ibid.*, Thomas Brotherton to Edward Allanson, 12 October 1695.

53 *Ibid.*, Francis Cholmondeley to Peter Legh, 29 September 1695.

54 *HMC Kenyon*, pp. 384–5; JRL, Legh MSS, corresp., Roger Kenyon to Peter Legh, 19 October 1695; Preston, Lancashire Archives, Kenyon MSS DDKe/9/68/81, Roger Kenyon to Sir John Ardern, 21 October 1695.

55 JRL, Legh MSS, corresp., John Grosvenor to Peter Legh, 14 October 1695; *ibid.*, Sir Thomas Grosvenor to Peter Legh, 15 October 1695; *ibid.*, Peter Legh to Sir Thomas Grosvenor [*c*.15 October 1695]; *ibid.*, James Shaen to Sir William Russell, 24 September 1695; *ibid.*, Sir William Russell to Elizabeth Legh, 8 October 1695; *ibid.*, Sir William Russell to Peter Legh, 22 October 1695.

56 London, British Library, Add. MS 36913, fols 232, 235; Kew, National Archives, SP 35/33/67.
57 JRL, Legh MSS, corresp., Edward Allanson to John Ward, 13 May 1708.
58 *Ibid.*
59 *London Gazette*, 14–17 October 1706, 20–23 September 1712, 23–27 June 1713.
60 JRL, Legh MSS, muniments box Y, address [*c.*1704–5].
61 *Ibid.*
62 *Ibid.*
63 JRL, Legh MSS, muniments box Z, Abraham Blackmore to Edward Allanson, 4 March 1714; *ibid.*, box Y, Abraham Blackmore to Thomas Legh, 11 March 1714.
64 Speck, *Tory and Whig*, pp. 25–8, 38–62; O'Gorman, *Voters, Patrons and Parties*, pp. 106–71.
65 JRL, Legh MSS, muniments box Z, anonymous account of 1685 election.
66 JRL, Legh MSS, box Z, Newton election expenses for 1685 and 1691; *ibid.*, box Y, Newton election expenses for 1722, 1734, 1741, 1747, 1754, 1761 and 1768.
67 *Ibid.*, corresp., J. Holcroft to Peter Steele, 20 May 1741.
68 The previous year, Ward had also ordered that '4 vessels at least of Ale be brewed at Newton' and distributed to the town: JRL, Legh MSS, corresp., John Ward to Peter Legh, 7 June 1712, 12 September 1712, 28 May 1713.
69 Chester, Cheshire Archives, Leicester-Warren MSS DLT/Adds. 5, Peter Legh to Sir Francis Leicester, 23 August 1720.
70 JRL, Legh MSS, corresp., Edward Allanson to Peter Legh, 24 July 1727. For evidence that such races continued into the 1740s, see *ibid.*, Legh Master to Peter Legh, 6 February 1742.
71 *Ibid.*, muniments box Z, Abraham Blackmore to Edward Allanson, 4 March 1714; *ibid.*, box Y, Blackmore to Thomas Legh, 11 March 1714.
72 JRL, Legh MSS, corresp., William Shippen to Peter Legh, 9 December 1714.
73 *Ibid.*, Francis Cholmondeley to Peter Legh, 23 August 1699; London, British Library, Add. MS 70020, fol. 120; London, British Library, Add. MS 29588, fols 68–9, 74–5, 78, 109–10, 140–1.
74 London, British Library, Lothian MSS, Lord Stanhope to Thomas Coke [*c.*1701].
75 *Historical Manuscripts Commission, Twelfth Report, Appendix, Part II The Manuscripts of the Earl Cowper* (London: Her Majesty's Stationery Office, 1888), 2, p. 421.
76 Handley, 'Lancashire', pp. 289–93.
77 JRL, Legh MSS, corresp., Peter Legh to John Ward [*c.*21 August 1713]; *ibid.*, muniments box Z, Ward to [Allanson], 28 August 1713; *ibid.*, Blackmore to [Allanson], 4 March 1714.
78 D. Szechi, 'The Tory Party in the House of Commons 1710–1714: A Case Study in Structural Change and Political Evolution', *Parliamentary History*, 5 (1986), 1–16.
79 JRL, Legh MSS, muniments box Y, Abraham Blackmore to Thomas Legh, 11 March 1714.
80 Clergy of the Church of England Database (https://theclergydatabase.org.uk/ [accessed 2 March 2024]), entry for Henry Finch (1789-28).
81 JRL, Legh MSS, muniments box Y, Blackmore to Thomas Legh, 11 March 1714.

82 Manchester, Greater Manchester Record Office, Legh MSS E17/89/1/7, Leicester to Peter Legh, 3 February 1715; JRL, Legh MSS, muniments box Z, Abraham Blackmore to Thomas Legh, 11 March 1714.

83 These comments are based on the biographies of Newton's Members published in Cruickshanks, Hayton and Handley, *House of Commons*.

84 JRL, Legh MSS, corresp., Bishop Thomas Cartwright to Richard Legh, 2 June 1687; muniments box U, depositions concerning Newton chapel, 3 Sept. 1733.

85 JRL, Legh MSS, corresp., Edward Allanson to Peter Legh, 24 July 1727.

86 JRL, Legh MSS, corresp., Thomas Brotherton to [Edward Allanson], 12 October 1695, Edward Allanson to John Ward, 13 May 1708; muniments box Z, John Ward to [Edward Allanson], 28 August 1713, Abraham Blackmore to Edward Allanson, 4 March 1714.

87 CA, Leicester-Warren MSS DLT/Adds. 5, Peter Legh to Sir Francis Leicester, 4 December [1720], 11 December 1720.

88 *Ibid.*, DLT/C35/5, same to same, 13 December 1723.

89 O'Gorman, *Voters, Patrons and Parties*, pp. 27-58; Porritt, *Unreformed House of Commons* I, 29-84.

90 O'Gorman, *Voters, Patrons and Parties*, pp. 31-2.

91 *Ibid.*, p. 34.

92 *Ibid.*, p. 37.

93 *Ibid.*

94 *Ibid.*, p. 38.

95 *Ibid.*, p. 43.

96 JRL, Legh MSS, muniments box Y, list of signatories to election return, 1768.

97 Speck, *Tory and Whig*, p. 57.

Longford Hall Revisited: A New Building Date, and an Architect

RICHARD BOND, ARCHIVES AND LOCAL STUDIES OFFICER, MANCHESTER CENTRAL LIBRARY (1991–2011)

Abstract

Much has been published about John Rylands, whether during his lifetime, in response to his death, or by historians looking back. While records of his business are plentiful, archival records for the Longford estate he bought in Stretford, Lancashire in 1855, including the hall he subsequently built, were not easily found. In recent years, however, estate records have emerged with new information, suggesting others may have survived. These records prompt a reassessment of the date at which Longford Hall was built, and identify the architect as Philip Nunn. This article explores Nunn's career, and his work as a leading architect is set in the context of the contemporary vogue for Italianate architecture, especially for warehouses. Longford Hall's demolition in 1995 was a major loss to Longford Park, but a more positive approach to the Park's history is in prospect, with a multi-million pound Lottery bid approved, and plans to catalogue Stretford's building plans.

Keywords: Longford Hall; John Rylands; Philip Nunn; warehouse; Italianate

Much has been written about John Rylands, both by his contemporaries following his death in 1888 and more recently, particularly by the textile historian Douglas Farnie.[1] This literature covers a wide range of subjects, including his business, his philanthropy, his interests in horticulture and books, and his family origins. In contrast, his purchase of the Longford estate in Stretford, Lancashire, in 1855 and the subsequent building of a new Longford Hall, replacing a previous mansion, has attracted very little attention. Even Farnie, in his book-length biography of Rylands, simply states that he 'made his home in 1857 in a new hall built in Italian style', before going on to discuss the landscaping of the estate in much more detail.[2] The 1857 date is widely cited, and seems to have been first published in the *In Memoriam* volume in 1889.[3] That volume and later printed sources do not name an architect. Indeed, English Heritage's submission to the 1994 inquiry into the proposed demolition of the Hall noted that 'it is surprising that no architect has been identified'.[4] In 2015, Trafford Local Studies drew my attention to some Longford Park records which had become available. These included a 1911 report by Stretford's borough surveyor, in a 'Longford Park Purchase' file, giving dates for various buildings, with the Hall dated as 1860–62.[5] Over the next five years, evidence emerged which suggested not only that the building date was indeed 1860–62, but that the architect was probably Philip Nunn, a significant but forgotten Manchester architect. In January 2021, I received an email from Trafford Local Studies, attaching a copy of a plan of the proposed bay windows for what was clearly Longford Hall (Figure 1) dated 1861 and signed by Philip Nunn (Figure 2), which finally confirmed that both propositions were correct.[6]

This article sets out the evidence for the dating as 1860–62, and explores how the date of 1857 came to be accepted. Accepting that revised dating requires, in turn, a reassessment of John Rylands's early years in Stretford, reinforcing the importance he attached to gardening, with the building of a new Hall a lesser priority, and the development of his Longford estate, drawing on previously unpublished material. Rylands's employment of Nunn is significant: Nunn had only started his practice two years earlier, and within five years he had gained a reputation as a leading architect in Manchester. Moreover, Nunn's name provides links to the wider picture of architectural developments in Manchester, and indeed to the role of an architect. Previously, only one commission was attributed to Nunn, but my research has identified two more, with Longford Hall being the earliest. It will be seen that his work was very much part of the Italianate style of architecture favoured in Manchester at the time. Nunn came to be recognised as a leading architect by his Manchester contemporaries, playing a key role in the creation of the Manchester Society of Architects. His career illustrates, however, the way in which architects of the time needed to supplement actual commissions with other sources of income, which in turn underlines that the architectural profession had yet to become fully developed.

These new discoveries also shed new light on the place of Longford Hall in the development of the estate, including the numerous houses and other structures that survive to this day and make up a significant part of the built environment of the Longford Park area in Stretford, and will inform how the site at Longford Park is managed in the future. Farnie's biography mentions the building of housing on the Longford estate itself, but the extensive purchases of land and houses immediately to the west is covered in just two sentences. The identification of Longford Hall's architect has come too late to be considered in the inquiry into its proposed demolition. While it is unlikely to have changed the outcome, this article examines whether the arguments against demolition were as effective as they might have been in the light of the new evidence.

Answering these questions prompts reflection on the importance of the interpretation of historical records, including those which have previously been overlooked for various reasons. It also highlights the significance of not only preserving but providing access to such records. The publication of this research comes at a doubly opportune time. Trafford Council has secured a multimillion-pound award from the National Lottery Heritage Fund for a range of improvements to Longford Park, including investment to secure the future of historic buildings and features and improving recreational options. Reinterpretation of the park's history will be a key part of the proposals (on which actual work should commence in 2024). Moreover, in July 2024 Trafford Local Studies are launching a project to catalogue a large collection of building plans, many of them for Stretford, and it is possible more plans of the Hall may be found, and also of other buildings associated with the

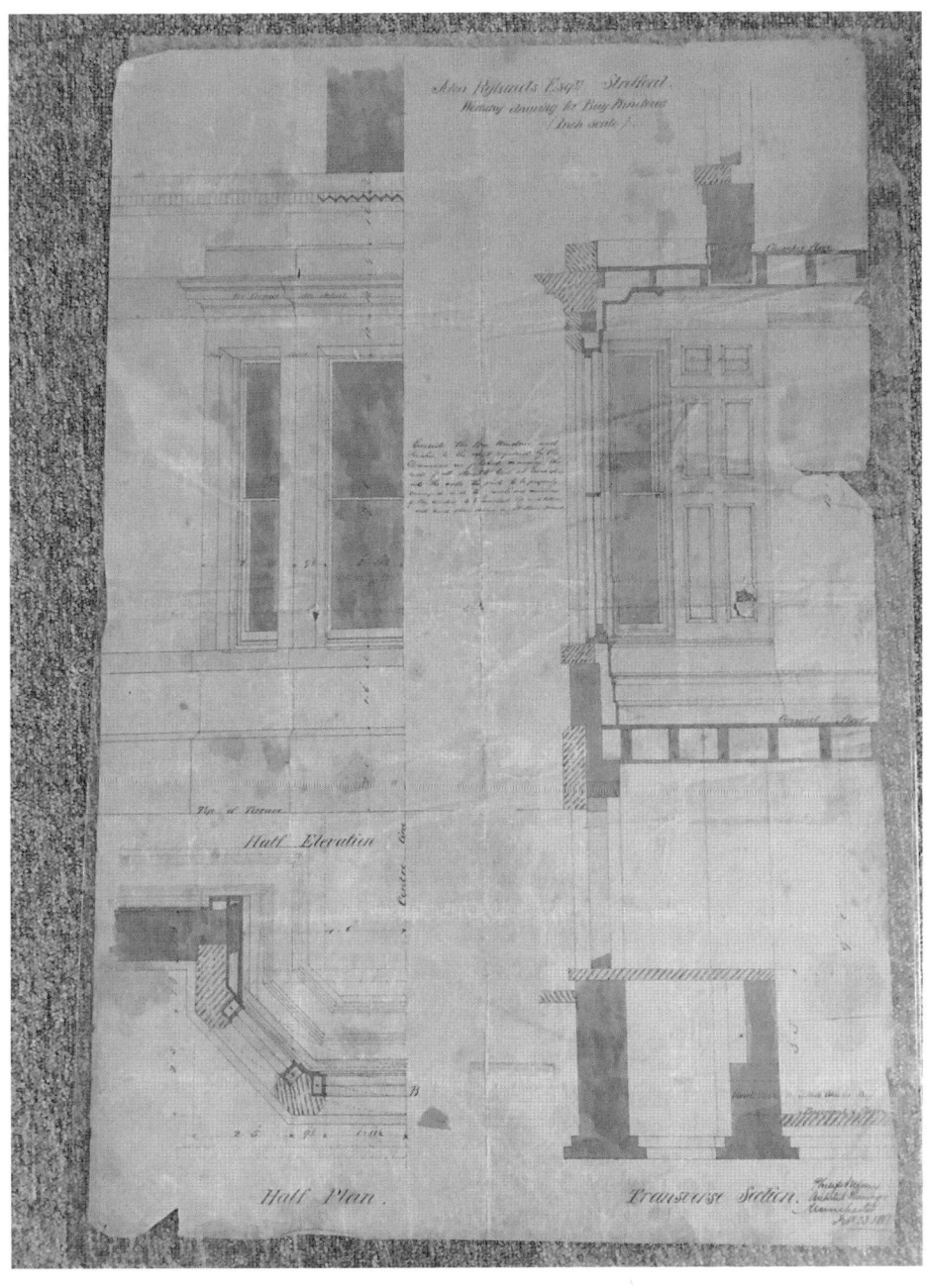

Figure 1 Building plan, 1861. Trafford Local Studies collection, cat. ref. PLA/1/786/1.

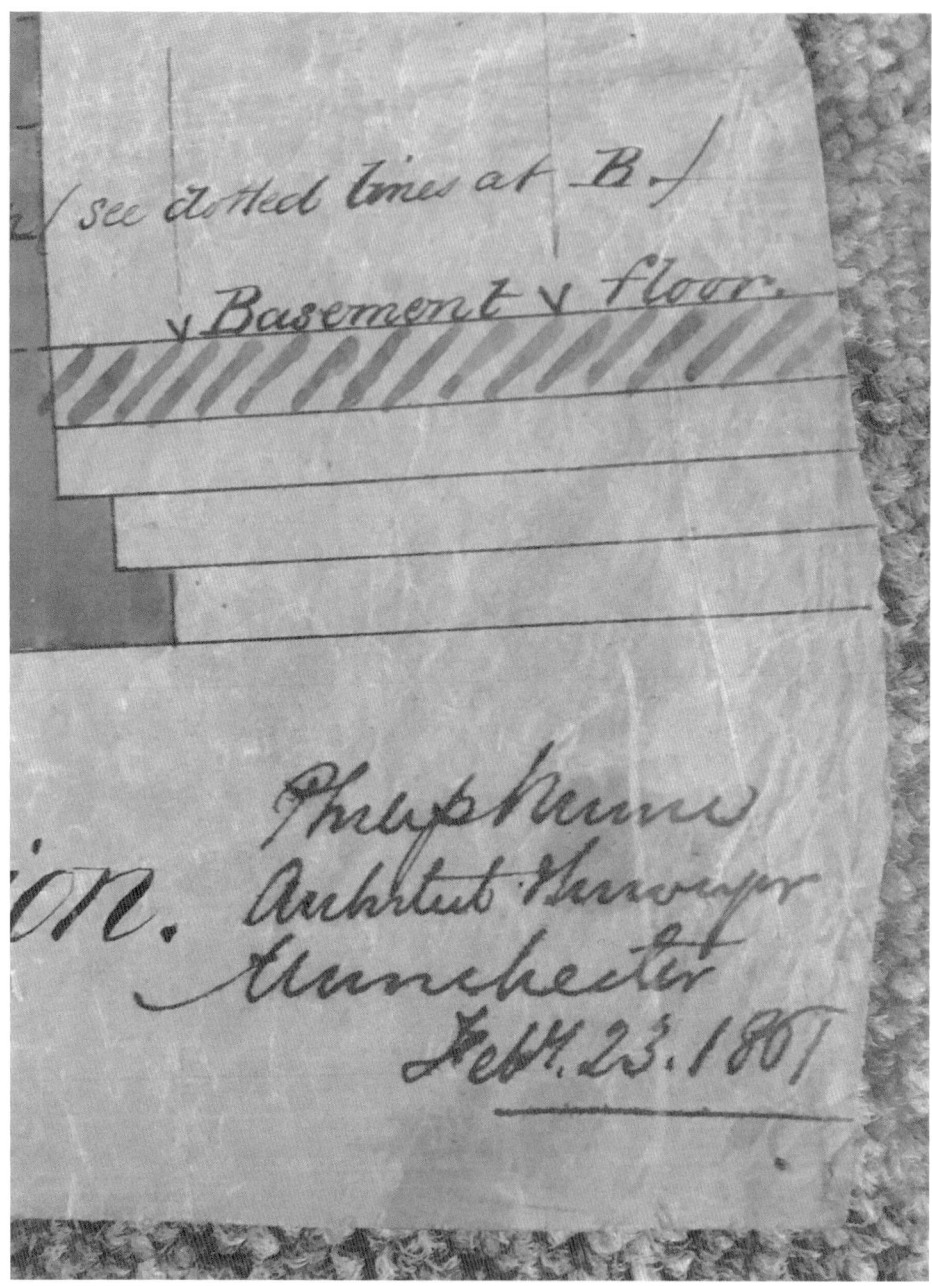

Figure 2 Close-up of Nunn's signature on the building plan, 1861. Trafford Local Studies collection, cat. ref. PLA/1/786/1.

Rylands family. It is to be hoped that the significance of this article's findings, and particularly of the role of Philip Nunn, can be incorporated into the future conservation plans for the management of the park.

Reassessing the Date

So how did a revised building date of 1860–62 emerge, and what evidence is there to support it? In 2013, a collection of Stretford Council records stored in the attic of Greater Manchester County Record Office was transferred to Trafford Local Studies. Knowing of my interest in the Longford estate, Trafford Local Studies contacted me in 2015 to say that they had prepared a box list of the records, which included some boxes relating to Longford Park. Although the Stretford collection catalogue (referenced as 'STR') can be found online, the box listing means that detail is limited. In the records, I found a file titled 'Longford Park Purchase'; this included a 1911 report by Stretford's Borough Surveyor on buildings to be retained, following Stretford Council's purchase of the estate. Building dates were given in most cases, and remarkably, the date given for Longford Hall was 1860–62.

As this clearly contradicted the accepted date of 1857, the question became how this might be tested, given the apparent lack of early sources. It seemed that there were no estate records which referenced the building date. There were no contemporary newspaper reports, although Clare Hartwell did point out that newspapers of the time are not usually helpful on private houses.[7] There was no reference to Longford Hall in *The Builder*, and nor did Edwin Waugh mention the estate in the Stretford part of his *Lancashire Sketches* of 1857. Detailed articles about the estate's conservatories were published in 1862[8] and 1875,[9] but neither refer to the building of the Hall. Surviving maps and plans did not appear to shed any light either. The 1838 Stretford tithe plan shows a farmhouse-type layout on the site,[10] while the 1845 Ordnance Survey 6-inch map, sheet 111, shows the Longford Hall erected by Charles James Stanley Walker – the building demolished by Rylands. The earliest estate plans – both surveyed by John Rylands's nephew John Spencer Raby – are dated 1881 and 1885.[11] Moreover, both building dates in question preceded the creation, in 1868, of the Stretford Local Board of Health – whose approval was needed for new buildings – while the earlier Stretford vestry minutes do not refer to the building of the Hall either.

One way forward would be to assess the accuracy of the other building dates given in the surveyor's report. The report is a little imprecise about the actual dating of two glass structures. A circular glass house is said to have been built 'about the same period as the Hall', but the earliest dating evidence found is in the 1881 estate plan.[12] The conservatory attached to the Hall is said to have been built about 1891. This would fit, as an earlier structure is shown on the estate plans of 1881 and 1885, but the distinctive shape of a new conservatory is shown on the first edition Ordnance Survey 25-inch map, sheet CXI.1, surveyed 1892.[13] The report is more precise about the dates of two estate buildings. The building used today as a cafe was, according to the 1911 report, originally used as estate offices and a dairy:

'a one-storey detached building containing a suite of rooms that have been mainly used as offices, and the back portion as a dairy … they were built in 1904'.[14] The 1904 Stretford committee minutes confirm the approval of a dairy for Mrs Rylands.[15] The farm buildings now referred to as the Shippon complex are said to be 'a quadrangular range of one-storey buildings round an open yard … They were built in 1898/9, and comprise Stables, Shippons, Tool Houses and the like'.[16] This date likewise tallies, as the buildings were the subject of a planning application in 1898.[17]

The report also describes residential properties on the estate. The report says the Sunnyside houses 'comprise a block of seven houses built in 1877, – a large three-storey one in the centre … and three smaller four-roomed houses on either side'.[18] There is no doubt about the 1877 date, which was recorded in stone on the houses' frontage. The report further describes eight workmen's cottages, known today as Longford Cottages; no date is given for the block of three houses and the detached house, but these are both known to be twentieth century. The report does, however, give a precise date for the older block of four cottages: 1871.[19] It is unfortunate that two building plans for these cottages – found in 2021 along with the 1861 plan of the Hall – are undated.[20] The plans were signed 'M. Lofthouse', and Michael Lofthouse certainly became John Rylands's steward in 1871 and is believed to have then moved into the largest of the four cottages. The block is shown on the 1881 estate plan, and significantly, the second 1875 *Gardener's Chronicle* article refers to these cottages as recently built to house eight of the workmen.[21] Moreover, the 1871 census, taken 2 April 1871, records three occupied gardeners' cottages, and five gardeners living in a bothy.[22]

Two residential properties which the report refers to are of particular significance in understanding when the Hall was built and who the architect was. The report states that the West Lodge – the building which still stands at the Edge Lane entrance to the park – was built at the same time as the Hall.[23] Although the lodge has in recent times been extended to the rear, it was clearly built in keeping with the architecture of the Hall, with its use of brick, stone dressings and slate roof. The report indicates that the building of the lodge was contemporaneous with that of the Hall, and is clear about the date the Hall was built: 'the major portion was erected in the years 1860/2 and there were extensions in 1892 and 1894'.[24] The suggestion of extensions at these later dates seems plausible, as Enriqueta Rylands (née Tennant) at that time was looking to expand her book collections. Indeed, in June 1892, she spent the then-astonishing sum of £210,000 on Earl Spencer's Althorp Library, which was transported in six hundred cases to the Hall, and remained there until the John Rylands Library opened some seven years later.[25] Work at the Hall on new shelves, electric lighting and a strongroom took place in 1892, and Trafford Local Studies have two building plans for that year, one showing the construction of a new billiard room.[26] The John Rylands Library has four undated building plans for alterations to the Hall; these were thought to date to 1892, but now seem more likely to date to 1894.[27]

Although the Borough Surveyor's report of 1911 was written some fifty years after the Hall was built, it therefore seems remarkably well-informed about the dates of the various estate buildings. How was this possible? A major clue is provided on the reverse of the 1861 Hall plan, which was stamped to affirm that it was received by Stretford Urban District Council, Surveyor's Office, 8 April 1911. It was in April 1911 that Stretford Council applied to the Local Government Board for borrowing powers to cover the £15,000 cost of the purchase (accompanied by the Surveyor's report, also dated April 1911) of the buildings to be retained. It seems highly likely Enriqueta's trustees would have passed over other plans too. Their minutes, dated 15 May 1908, record that books and papers relating to the estate had been placed in a strong room at Longford Hall, pending a decision on their disposal.[28]

What other evidence is there to indicate that the surveyor's dating of the Hall is correct? Rate books offer tantalising clues. They certainly confirm that John Rylands moved to take up residence on the Longford estate in 1857, which in turn suggests he must have initially moved into the mansion built by Charles James Stanley Walker. The Ardwick rate book for 1856 records John Rylands owning and occupying 24 Ardwick Green, while the one for 1857 has the abbreviation 'E' – which clearly stands for empty – in the occupier column, though Rylands remained the owner.[29] Definite proof of his moving out of 24 Ardwick Green is provided by an advert offering the property to let, with immediate possession, dated 7 February 1857.[30] There are no Stretford rate books before 1858, but the one for 1858–59 shows John Rylands in residence.[31] The Chorlton rate books imply a change on the Longford estate around 1860–61, as the location of John Rylands's property is given as Chorlton-cum-Hardy in the rate books of 1858, 1859 and 1860, but as 'Nr Longford Hall' in 1861, 1862 and 1863.[32] Regrettably, the Stretford rate book series has many gaps: the earliest rate book is that for 1858–59, followed by 1860–61 and then 1866.[33] For these rate books, however, the rental value is suggestive: the first two quote a gross estimated rental for Longford Hall of £427 7s 0d, while the 1866 book shows that this had increased to £500.

Although John Rylands took up residence on the Longford estate in 1857, the evidence suggests that his initial preoccupation was with the development of the estate itself. As Farnie put it, 'extensive gardens and conservatories were laid out on the pattern of Chatsworth'.[34] A two-part article in a gardening journal of 1862 unfortunately made no reference to the Hall itself – indeed, the only building explicitly referred to as being built for John Rylands was a bothy, 'lodging-rooms' for his gardeners.[35] The author of the article made clear how extensive the conservatories were, however, comprising fourteen in total with three-quarters of an acre under glass, and also made clear that the buildings were finished to a very high standard. Although the previous owner of the estate, Charles James Stanley Walker, had been a keen gardener, he had fallen into financial difficulty in around 1845, and had to give up the estate on becoming insolvent in 1854.[36] It therefore seems highly likely that the extensive conservatories described in 1862 were erected for John Rylands. Local rate books suggest that this was indeed the case. As the estate included part of Chorlton-cum-Hardy as well as Stretford, John Rylands was recorded as the owner of land in Chorlton in the rate books of 1856 and 1857.[37] He had already made his mark on the estate by the time of the rate book of 1858, as he was then liable in respect of 'land, greenhouse and part of large greenhouse'.[38] This formula was repeated in every extant rate book until his death in 1888 (and indeed, beyond). Clearly, the greenhouses described in 1862 had been built on such an extensive scale as to extend over the township boundary.

Moreover, it may or may not be coincidence, but title deed evidence shows that a substantial terrace of six houses, still standing today and called Rivington Place, was built for John Rylands in 1862, located on the western boundary of his estate.[39] Much of the land to the west of the Longford estate had been sold off by Stephen Raingill from 1851.[40] This included a northern area of 16 acres sold to the Manchester and Northern Counties Freehold Land Society, which divided it into 160 building plots, which in turn were sold to individuals.[41] John Rylands's son William bought plots 81 and 82 in 1857, but when he died 27 November 1861, John Rylands used those plots and adjacent ones he had purchased to build Rivington Place.[42] It is unusual for title deeds to give an actual building date, but examination of the deeds for one of the houses revealed a statutory declaration dated 28 September 1909, by James Jones, who had then been the surveyor of the Longford estate for about twelve years, and who had become Enriqueta's private secretary.[43] Jones declared that the six houses numbered 58, 60, 62, 64, 66 and 68 Cromwell Street (re-named Cromwell Road in 1911) were built in 1862 on behalf of John Rylands, basing this in part on rental books. Much of the western boundary of the Longford estate was not built on until the twentieth century, but in this case it may be that the terrace was built as a screen for the Hall, and in particular the outbuildings that were built to the west and north of the Hall, which were already in existence according to an 1862 gardening article.[44] Rivington Place was built next to a slightly earlier terrace of three houses, called Trafford View, which were under construction in 1855.[45] Together, the nine houses did provide a substantial screen.

Before the 1861 Hall plan came to light, the most telling documentary evidence in support of the Hall being dated 1860–62 was the discovery among the Orford Papers of an 1860 plan, referred to here as the Orford plan.[46] The plan shows the 'site of lodge' at the corner of Edge Lane and Parker Street (now Cromwell Road) and a 'roadway to Longford Hall' starting from that junction and going past the site of the lodge. Given that the lodge and Hall, as built, shared the same styling – suggesting they were built about the same time – the dating of the lodge (and new entrance) is particularly significant. As the 1845 Ordnance Survey 6-inch map shows, the earlier main entrance to the Longford estate was not at the present lodge entrance from Edge Lane but further east, roughly halfway along the present stone wall fronting Edge Lane.

The Index to Deeds and Documents for the Longford Hall Estate records how the land for the lodge came to be incorporated into the estate.[47] In 1852, Stephen Raingill conveyed land comprising approximately 2993 square yards to Joseph Bancroft. John Rylands purchased the land from Bancroft on 27 March 1860, and the following day Raingill and another gave Rylands a 'Grant and Privilege' to erect a lodge thereon. The next day, the Stretford surveyors of the highways certified the Orford plan, as shown on the original plan and as recorded in the Index to Deeds and Documents. Clearly, the architect who drew up the Orford plan did so in the knowledge that a new access point was to be created, resulting in a new driveway to the Hall, and that a new lodge was to be built. Indeed, just a year later, the 1861 census shows the lodge was already occupied.[48] Given that relatively few estate records survive, and that the plans that do are not generally signed, it is remarkable that the Orford plan, dated 28 March 1860, was signed 'Philip Nunn Architect & Surveyor Manchester' (Figure 3) – just as he had signed the Hall plan dated eleven months later.

It is therefore instructive to consider how the building date came to be universally stated as 1857. The *In Memoriam* volume of 1889 is quite clear on the matter: it states that John Rylands bought the estate in 1855 and, having taken down the old Hall, he erected a mansion 'on which he entered in 1857'.[49] Later publications clearly relied on this information: the third volume of Crofton's three-volume history of Stretford, for example, published in 1903, virtually paraphrased the same statement.[50] Pevsner quoted 1857 as the date for the Hall, as did Farnie.[51] The key to understanding the *In Memoriam* date lies in considering who was responsible

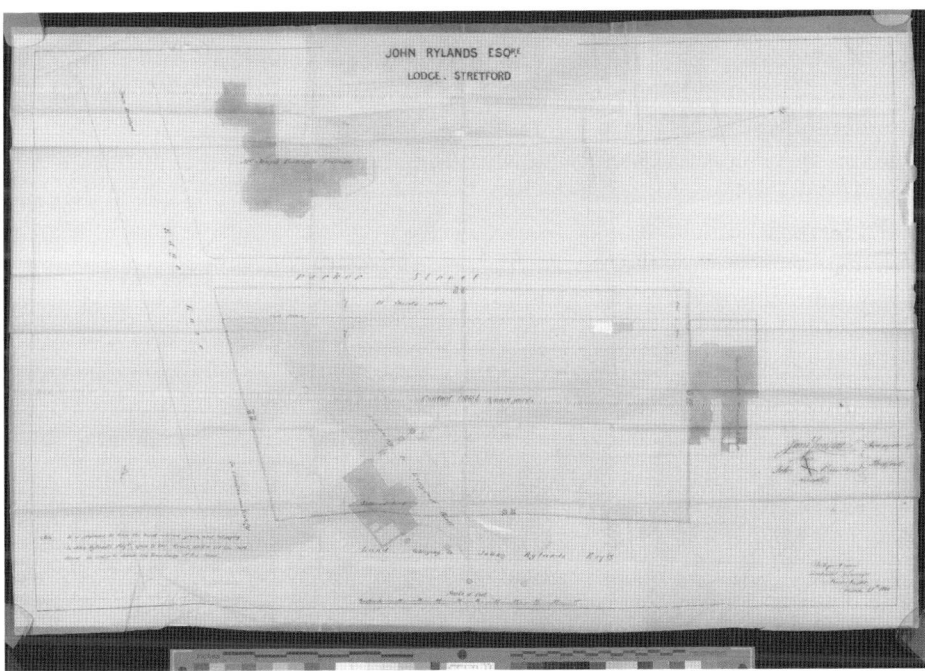

Figure 3 Plan of lodge for John Rylands, 1860. John Rylands Library (ORF/3/2/7). Copyright © The University of Manchester Library.

for producing that text. Farnie stated that Enriqueta Rylands encouraged Dr S. G. Green, a Baptist minister, to compose a memoir of her husband.[52] As can be seen in the *Oxford Dictionary of National Biography* entry for Samuel Gosnell Green, he had no particular connection to Stretford.[53] He was based in Bradford from 1851 and moved to London in 1876, where he remained until his death in 1905. As a biblical scholar and hymnologist, he was known to John Rylands, who possessed books written by him.[54] According to Farnie, Green also influenced Rylands' religious thinking. There is no evidence, however, that he knew John Rylands in 1857. Indeed, his relationship with the family came much later, in particular through becoming an adviser of Enriqueta Rylands following her husband's death in 1888. It seems probable that a key source of Green's information would have been Enriqueta Rylands herself. Enriqueta had no connection with Longford Hall in 1857, though, or indeed during 1860–62. According to Farnie, Enriqueta completed her education in Paris and London.[55] He suggests that she was not on the list of members of Stretford Congregational Church in 1862, and infers that she may have become a companion to the second Mrs Rylands in 1863; she did not marry John Rylands until 1875, following the death of his second wife. It is clear, then, that neither of the prime movers behind the memorial volume had first-hand knowledge of John Rylands or his Longford estate in 1857, or indeed during 1860–62.

The Forgotten Architect

So who was Philip Nunn, why might John Rylands have employed him as the architect of the Hall, and how did the design of the Hall come about? We should first consider how the architectural profession developed in Manchester. Outside London, the profession emerged slowly during the first half of the nineteenth century. Major provincial towns experiencing industrial expansion created demand, given the large number of buildings required and money available to pay for them, with merchants leading the way, having a need for large buildings but also vying to demonstrate the prosperity of their businesses. As *The Builder* put it in 1845, 'a new school of architects has sprung up [in Manchester], many of them young men, and it is greatly to the credit of the merchants of the town that they have had the judgement to use the services of architects'.[56] The development of the profession was fitful, though. Although Richard Lane established himself as a leading architect in Manchester in the 1820s and 1830s, he had to take on a variety of work.[57] Lane founded an architectural society in Manchester in 1837, but this only lasted until 1842.[58] In 1860, the Manchester Architectural Association was founded, but it was the creation of the Manchester Society of Architects in 1865 that marked a step change in the profile of the profession.

Philip Nunn (1830–67), although little known today, became a leading architect in Manchester, and his main claim to fame is arguably that he was a founding member of the Manchester Society of Architects. In the spring of 1865, Isaac Holden called a meeting of the leading architects in Manchester to discuss professional issues.[59] This meeting was held at the Clarence Hotel on 8 April 1865, with ten architects in attendance, one of whom was Nunn. The meeting agreed to appoint a committee to consider the formation of a society of architects, and the committee's report was considered at another meeting on 20 June 1865, which became the inaugural meeting of the Manchester Society of Architects. Philip Nunn was one of just nineteen founder members.[60] He was evidently an active member, being one of a committee of five who made representations to a government inquiry in 1866 on Manchester's introduction of new by-laws.[61] He was elected to the Society's Council – for a second time – at the annual meeting held on 24 June 1867.[62]

Despite this, no obituary has been traced for him, although this may partly be because of his early death in 1867. The Society's annual report did note his death, however: 'the Council regrets having to record the decease of two members, that of Philip Nunn (alluded to in the address of the President of the year), having occurred on the 10th August 1867, and more recently that of W. Mangnall, on the 29th May 1868. The former was an active working member of the Council.'[63] The report went on to say that although three new members had been elected, 'all must regret the loss of those who were so prominently connected with the origin and progress of the Society'.[64] Regrettably, the president's address has not survived in the Manchester Society of Architects' archives. It was published in *The Builder*, however, and it concluded with this tribute to Nunn by the president, William Reid Corson: 'the first breach by the hand of death has been made in our society, and the suddenness of the stroke, with the comparative youth of the member, adds to our sorrow. Your election of Philip Nunn to the council of the society in two successive years marked your appreciation of his character, and a business rapidly increasing testified to the satisfaction with which his work was regarded by his clients.'[65]

It seems that Nunn's business was indeed thriving, judging by the evidence of Manchester rate books. The annual rental for his offices at 71 Princess Street was £80 from 1859, but from 1865 the annual rental for 69, 71 and 73 Princess Street was £300.[66] From 1866, he occupied a house at 194 Oxford Road, for which the rental was £100, increasing to £110 in 1867.[67] When probate was granted on 29 August 1867, his effects including leaseholds were valued at under £10,000.[68] His sister Marianne Nunn, his sole beneficiary and executrix, then arranged for Messrs Royle and Bennett to take on his business as architect and surveyor.[69] More than thirty years later, the obituaries of both men referenced their employment by Nunn and, in the case of Bennett, made specific reference to the fact that Nunn, who as 'an architect though young in years, had, at the date of his death, made a considerable reputation'.[70]

It is interesting to consider what this reputation was based on. The editor of Nunn's entry on the Architects of Greater Manchester website, Neil Darlington, reports that few architects of the Victorian period could make the profession pay, and so sought additional income working as surveyors, estate agents and land developers.[71] This was evidently the case with Nunn, whose entries in trade directories state 'architect (and valuer)'. Having trained as an architect, he took control of the practice of the late Charles Lee, architect and surveyor, in 1858.[72] Between then and 1867, his name featured in many and varied newspaper adverts, some in connection with Daniel Bradshaw, an auctioneer whose business had been established in 1840.[73] Nunn had taken over Lee's practice in June 1858 and, not long after, Bradshaw advertised a public competition for the Monsall House estate with Philip Nunn, surveyor, one of several people from whom particulars could be obtained.[74] Other Bradshaw adverts that named Nunn as a contact person include several in 1866, including for the sale of a variety of properties on the banks of the Irwell in Salford, for building materials at the Talbot Hotel, Market Street, and for materials in a warehouse at the corner of Mosley Street and Booth Street.[75] Nunn also placed adverts directly, again for a variety of purposes. An early venture in his name was advertised in 1859, in which he proposed to lay out 42 acres, part of the Hope estate in Eccles, in plots for villa residences, although the main development of the area came much later.[76] Most of the adverts in Nunn's name date to 1864 onwards, and advertised actual properties such as 'wharves works and cottages near Windsor Bridge'.[77] Most related to Manchester warehouses, including two sites for new warehouses. They also included existing warehouses, including two or more in Bloom Street, 'which will be altered to suit tenants'.[78] It seems there was very little work he could claim responsibility for when he was taken on by Rylands, however; his most notable commission, for the building often referred to as the Behrens Warehouse, was slightly later than that for Longford Hall. His role within the Manchester Society of Architects, and an additional warehouse commission which can now be attributed to him, both came some five years later.

Nunn's entry on the Architects of Greater Manchester website states that his only known commission was the Behrens Warehouse, 127–133 Portland Street and 61 Oxford Street, and that 'references to his architectural work remain elusive'.[79] The entry can now be revised, since it is apparent that Nunn was responsible for the new Longford Hall, and was also the architect of a second warehouse. This became evident in earlier research on Nunn,[80] which also proved that the so-called Behrens Warehouse, said to have been built for Louis Behrens & Son, was originally built for Heugh & Balfour, as seen in a building plan Nunn signed and dated 17 September 1860.[81] More information has since come to light on how the Behrens Warehouse came to be built, via a newspaper advert, which reads 'Shipping warehouses – The owners of a plot of land, in Portland Street, are willing to erect warehouses thereon, to suit merchants – apply to Mr Philip Nunn'.[82] The resulting warehouse, at 127–133 Portland Street and 71 Oxford Street, was originally occupied by Heugh & Balfour, who specialised in the Indian trade. A similar advert was published regarding the warehouse that was to be built at the corner of John Dalton Street and Ridgefield, which can also now be credited to Nunn. The advert states that the owner of a plot of land in Ridgefield, about 186 square yards, 'is willing to ERECT a WAREHOUSE thereon, to suit a tenant', with application to be made to Philip Nunn.[83] Nunn's building plan is dated 10 August 1865, and is annotated to show that it was approved by the Improvements Committee on 28 August 1865.[84] Ordnance Survey 25-inch maps, sheet CIV.10, show that this was built, but replaced by a larger building between 1905 and 1915.

Why, then, did John Rylands choose Nunn as the architect to design a new Longford Hall? It was Nunn's earliest known commission, less than two years after Nunn had acquired Charles Lee's practice in June 1858. Moreover, Nunn did not seem to cultivate publicity about his activities; indeed, the only reason we know that he acted as architect and surveyor for the de Trafford estate is because, following his death, an advert was published stating that Mr W. M. Smith had been appointed as his successor in that role.[85] We can only speculate whether Sir Humphrey de Trafford recommended him to John Rylands, or vice versa, or indeed whether Rylands came across Nunn in some other way. Nunn's low profile, which suggests that he was a man of discretion, bears comparison with John Rylands himself, who never took up office in local or national affairs, and who, moreover, seemed keen to avoid publicity for both his business and philanthropy. Gardening was an exception, and something he clearly took a great interest in, but this did not impact the privacy surrounding his business affairs; extensive accounts of his horticultural activities were published in gardening journals in 1862 and 1875, and the Longford estate was entered in various horticultural competitions.[86] A rare exception to Rylands' low profile came in 1865, when he chaired a public meeting called to protest against a court decision to allow foul water to be admitted to canals, a decision which may have impacted the canal feeder which crossed his estate.[87]

What does seem clear, however, is that Rylands preferred to deal with people he knew and could rely on. His trusted business managers included William Carnelley, who first joined the firm in 1840 and rose to become one of nine directors when Rylands & Sons Ltd was established as a joint stock company in 1873. Reuben Spencer had first joined the firm in 1847, become a director in 1867, and then a director of Rylands & Sons Ltd in 1873. He employed Michael Lofthouse to act as his estate agent, certainly from 1871 to 1883, since this is the date range for a series of adverts by Mr Lofthouse for properties to rent, published in the *Manchester Guardian*.[88] The address at first is given as 'Garden Place, Nr Longford Hall', thought to be the largest of the four cottages built in 1871, and later as Estate Office, Longford Hall. His first name is not given, but is recorded in the 1881 census.[89] Michael's son, William Alfred Lofthouse, was a Manchester architect who had commenced independent practice in 1874. He has only two known commissions, a school in Stand, Whitefield (near Bury) in 1874, followed by a major commission when John Rylands entrusted him with the design of the Stretford Town Hall. This opened in 1879 and is still in existence today, now known as Stretford Public Hall, a prominent local landmark.[90]

The outcome of Nunn's commission for Longford Hall was not the imposing mansion that might have been expected of such a wealthy man. When the John Rylands Library opened in 1899, Joseph Parker referred to Longford Hall as an 'unpretentious but comfortable house'.[91] In 1994, English Heritage described it as 'a suburban villa writ large, as befitted its owner, in a competent if not very inspiring Italianate style with the inevitable embellishments of bay windows'. Another Italianate feature was a hidden roof.[92] John Rylands's choice of style for his house must surely have been influenced by the prevalence of Italianate architecture in Victorian Manchester, particularly in warehouses.

The Florence of the Nineteenth Century

Frank Salmon suggested that the term 'Italianate' encompasses a number of genres, with the palazzo mode on which Manchester warehouses were often based simply being one of these.[93] Charles Barry's Manchester Athenaeum (now part of the Art Gallery) is said to have paved the way in 1837, but Edward Walters's warehouse for Richard Cobden at 14–16 Mosley Street was the first Manchester warehouse to adopt the palazzo style; this then became the dominant style for commercial warehouses for the next thirty to forty years.[94] Impressive warehouses were built in the commercial district spanning Mosley Street, Portland Street and Princess Street, with Nunn's Portland Street warehouse an example. Manchester merchants seemed to readily identify with medieval and Renaissance Florence and the palazzo style architecture associated with it: at the 1875 general meeting of the Manchester Society of Architects, the president Thomas Worthington referred to Manchester as 'the inland metropolis of the North – the Florence, if I may so describe it, of the nineteenth century'.[95] The Italianate style was likewise adopted for other Manchester buildings, such as offices, banks and baths, creating new variations in style. This also became the case for warehouse buildings in the 1850s, not least because practical issues led to variations in the earlier formulas of design. H.-R. Hitchcock suggested that the wide spacing of windows required by correct palazzo precedent was awkward for offices requiring maximum light, and that the model palazzo was only three storeys high, while the rising value sites in urban business districts meant that office buildings often carried to four or five storeys high.[96]

As Manchester merchants clearly favoured the style, whether for aesthetic or practical reasons (or both), it is perhaps not surprising that John Rylands chose to have his hall built in the same style. It may be significant that he employed an architect who subsequently had two other commissions, from other clients, both being for warehouses which were Italianate in style. Indeed, and rather curiously, the 1865 plan of Nunn's warehouse on the corner of John Dalton Street and Ridgefield looks very much like a five-storey version of Longford Hall.[97] Nevertheless, while the Italianate style was in vogue at the time for warehouses, this was not as true for domestic architecture, in which other styles such as Grecian and Gothic were also favoured. The term 'Italianate' was first used in reference to domestic houses in the early nineteenth century, with Cronkhill House being seen as the pioneer and Queen Victoria's Osborne House as the apogee.[98] Both typically omitted pillars and columns, but included a belvedere tower. Italianate villas were by no means consistent in style, however – Longford Hall certainly had no tower, for example. N. Pevsner noted a good number of surviving examples in the Liverpool area and one at St Helens, but only identified four in what is now the Greater Manchester area: Longford Hall, Greygarth Hall in Victoria Park, a terrace in Whalley Range, and the villa that became Mossley Town Hall (now a private residence again). While Italianate warehouses found favour in part for practical reasons, such considerations did not apply to domestic buildings; John Rylands could have chosen to have his home built in another style, such as Grecian or Gothic, which suggests he chose Italianate for aesthetic reasons. Indeed, some years later – from 1866, according to Farnie – he took a greater interest in Italy in general.[99]

Changing Attitudes to Longford Park's History and Heritage

Having identified the architect of the Hall and established that Nunn only has three known commissions, it is even more regrettable that Longford Hall was almost entirely demolished in 1995, leaving only one of Nunn's buildings to survive intact. The Hall had seen a variety of uses since Longford Park opened in 1912, including accommodation for Belgian refugees, a Red Cross hospital, a museum and art gallery, and a variety of municipal and community functions. In 1977, it hosted the only royal garden party to be held outside London, but in 1983 it was closed because of repair problems. Trafford Council eventually proposed to demolish it, leading to an inquiry in 1994 and its subsequent demolition. Its end is still very much a talking point among Stretford people.

It is instructive to look again at the arguments presented at the 1994 inquiry for what they reveal about attitudes towards the historical significance of Longford Hall and the role of historical research in reinterpreting our understanding of cultural heritage. The arguments advanced in 1994 revolved chiefly around how important a figure John Rylands was, rather than the significance of the Hall itself, while the importance of Enriqueta Rylands seemed to pass unnoticed. Possibly prompted by Pevsner's reference to its 'indifferent Italianate style', the tone was set by the English Heritage listing of the Hall in 1988, which noted that the 'principal significance' of the Hall was its status as the former home of John Rylands, as quoted in a 1994 statement supplied by Frank Kelsall of English Heritage to the inquiry.[100] It was Frank Kelsall's eight-page statement which contained the description of the Hall as a 'suburban villa writ large' and of it being built in a 'competent if not very inspiring Italianate style'.[101] It also stated that 'the hall is still recognisably the house which Rylands built, albeit extended, much municipalised within and now somewhat derelict'.[102] This description was hardly a compelling argument for retention. Moreover, the statement acknowledged that the Hall's architect was unknown, which is unfortunate given the interest in Nunn as an architect to which this article has drawn attention. The report nevertheless tried to broaden the argument about the significance of the Hall by noting that 'Longford Hall represents a type recently identified by George Sheeran in West Yorkshire as *Brass Castles*, that is the suburban or country homes of rich businessmen'.[103] It went on to assert that English Heritage believed 'that Longford Hall is properly listed as a Grade II building, in its own right as [a] piece of mid-Victorian architecture, through its associations with a major historical figure and as a representative as a building type'.[104]

Farnie's submission to the inquiry seems to have paid little attention to the significance of the Hall as a building. Mark Lowe KC, of Gray's Inn, acted for the council at the inquiry, and his closing submission contended that 'Dr F refers to LH on only two or three occasions in his 103 pages'.[105] Farnie's arguments for retention of the Hall revolved very much around its association with John Rylands, although his thinking on this seems to have shifted by the time of the inquiry. He had written a letter on 27 July 1993, addressed to the Secretary of State for the Environment and the chairman of English Heritage, making a reasoned plea for retention on the basis of the association of the Hall and estate with three figures of national importance: Thomas Walker, John Rylands and Enriqueta Rylands.[106] However, in a handwritten summary of his evidence dated 5 April 1994, Farnie wrote: 'I consider that Longford Hall is a building of exceptional historical importance because of its historical association with John Rylands.'[107] Farnie perhaps focused almost exclusively on the importance of the Hall's link to John Rylands because he had taken exception to the view of Rylands presented in a 1992 report commissioned by Trafford Council from Hammond Suddards Research and written by their Bradford-based consultant John Ayers.[108] Ayers's report downplayed John Rylands's significance, asserting that he 'was not an inventor, an innovator, an entrepreneur, a philanthropist or one who used his powers for the public good. He was not, in my view, a great man.'[109] This report prompted a 24-page rebuttal by Farnie.[110] He listed various allegations by Ayers and set out arguments against these, for example, that 'his philanthropic activities were not in any way exceptional'.[111] Farnie also took issue with Ayers's use of sources, noting that he had failed to reference Sutton's 1897 article in the *Dictionary of National Biography*, and that he had made very selective use of his earlier biography of John Rylands.[112] Mark Lowe's 1994 submission in turn suggested that Farnie took an almost proprietorial sense of the significance of John Rylands, based on some forty years of study, and that this had resulted in a 'marked lack of objectivity' on Farnie's part.[113] Some years later, Farnie suggested that the arguments about the importance of John Rylands illustrated the Wiener thesis, which focused on the low status ascribed to businessmen in British society.[114]

Perhaps the most surprising feature of the inquiry – given the focus on John Rylands – is the relative absence of reference to Enriqueta Rylands. Enriqueta's life is now much better known, and her achievements recognised. In 2004 Farnie wrote an article about her for the *Oxford Dictionary of National Biography*, while Elizabeth Gow curated an exhibition on her at the John Rylands Library in 2008. Gow has also completed a 2023 PhD thesis on Enriqueta, and a Stretford street was recently named Enriqueta Rylands Close.[115] Farnie had previously published a whole article devoted to Enriqueta in 1989, which makes her effective absence from the inquiry rather surprising and, with hindsight, regrettable.[116] Much might have been made of her significance as a person in her own right, but also of the close connections between Longford Hall and the library she founded in her husband's name. She started purchasing books for the project in 1889, but it would be ten years before the library actually opened; the purchase of the Althorp Library in 1892 thus prompted major changes to accommodate it at the hall, including the creation of a basement strongroom.[117] Since an 1892 building plan includes provision for a 'new billiard room', it may be that a billiard room was previously located in the basement.[118] In 1901, she bought the Crawford Collection as part of her private library and initially kept this at the Hall as well, until the trustees of the John Rylands Library persuaded her to transfer it there in 1903.

Its demolition in 1995 was not the last of the story of the Hall and its surroundings. A positive step came in 1996 with the designation of a Longford Conservation Area by Trafford Council. In 1999, the fate of the Hall and apparent neglect of the park led a group of local residents to form the Friends of Longford Park, a group which aims at seeking park improvements. The Friends group remains very active, and was highly supportive of the council's recent National Lottery Heritage Fund bid for Longford Park. In September 2023, it was announced that the bid, for £3.1 million, had succeeded, which will form part of a £6.1 million investment in the park. The proposed changes will include various historical angles, including a clearer interpretation of the floor layout of the Hall, and exposing the whole of the Hall frontage to view; this all survives to the ground-floor windowsill level, but one side is completely hidden by vegetation at present. Meanwhile, Trafford Council have secured funding for Trafford Local Studies to catalogue a huge collection of the building plans transferred to them some two years ago. It is possible that more Nunn plans may be found – it seems unlikely that only one was handed to Stretford Council in 1911 – but certainly plans of the many properties in Stretford associated with John and Enriqueta Rylands are likely to surface. In another positive development, a local resident, David Brady, is working up a comprehensive gazetteer of the historic houses on the west side of the park, many built or bought by John Rylands, which currently runs to more than 400 pages.[119]

Conclusion

The revised building date for Longford Hall provides us with a better understanding of John Rylands's early years in Stretford, with priority given to gardening rather than building at first. It demonstrates the value of questioning historical sources – *In Memoriam* should now be treated with caution – while the 1911 surveyor's report provides a much more accurate account of the development of the estate. Indeed, the crucial importance of primary sources is evident from the fact that building plans confirm that Philip Nunn was the architect chosen by John Rylands to build a hall and remodel his estate. Nunn's career was short, but he made a crucial contribution to the burgeoning architectural profession in Manchester, while his known commissions – all Italianate – suggest that style was still popular, and indeed was appreciated by John Rylands. The research has also highlighted other sources previously overlooked, or whose significance has been understated: for example, the *Index to Deeds and Documents* provides a detailed record of all the land and property purchased by Rylands to the west of his estate, and cross-references the building plots shown on the 1885 estate plan, which are not shown on the 1881 plan.

Title deeds provide another potential source of information. It is hoped that this article will enable the Lottery project to bring into sharper focus the history of the Hall and its estate, and the estate's impact on Stretford as a whole, and inform the future management of the park and its surroundings. Moreover, the sources explored open up the prospect of a major reassessment of the Rylands era in Stretford.

Acknowledgements

Many have assisted my research, but particular thanks go to Neil Darlington for his architectural knowledge and for not updating his Nunn article on the website 'A Biographical Dictionary of the Architects of Greater Manchester 1800–1940', pending publication of this study, and to Elizabeth Gow and John Hodgson for their invaluable assistance.

Notes

1. Farnie's contribution, besides his articles on John Rylands and Enriqueta Rylands for the *Oxford Dictionary of National Biography* (Oxford: Oxford University Press, 2004), includes the following: D. A. Farnie, 'John Rylands of Manchester', *Bulletin of the John Rylands Library*, 75:2 (1993), 3–103; D. A. Farnie, 'Enriqueta Augustina Rylands, 1843–1908, Founder of the John Rylands Library', *Bulletin of the John Rylands Library*, 71:2 (1989), 3–38; D. A. Farnie, 'The Wiener Thesis Vindicated: The Onslaught of 1994 upon the Reputation of John Rylands of Manchester', in D. Jeremy, *Religion, Business and Wealth in Modern Britain* (London: Routledge, 1998), pp. 86–107; D. A. Farnie, 'Money-making and Charitable Endeavour: John and Enriqueta Rylands of Manchester', *The Journal of the United Reformed Church History Society*, 6 (2000), 429–38.
2. Farnie, 'John Rylands', 19.
3. [S. G. Green], *In Memoriam John Rylands, Born February 7, 1801, Died December 11, 1888* (printed for private circulation, Manchester, 1889): https://catalog.hathitrust.org/Record/008399743 [accessed 2 October 2023].
4. Manchester, John Rylands Library, Douglas Farnie Papers, DFP box 2/5 (temporary reference), file 're. 1994 inquiry and Longford Hall demolition', English Heritage Statement, 1994, p. 2.
5. Sale, Trafford Local Studies, STR/1/12/19/1 box 3 of 3, file 'Longford Park Purchase', containing 'Surveyor's Report of Buildings Proposed to be Retained (April 1911)', by Ernest Worrall.
6. Sale, Trafford Local Studies, PLA/1/786/1, building plan, 23 February 1861.
7. Personal communication by email, 6 January 2020.
8. T. Appleby, 'Longford Hall', *Journal of Horticulture and Cottage Gardener*, 47 (28 January 1862), 353–4: https://biodiversitylibrary.org/page/25660025, and 47 (18 February 1862), 417–18: https://biodiversitylibrary.org/page/25660089 [both accessed 2 October 2023].

9 T. Baines, 'Longford Hall, Stretford', *Gardener's Chronicle*, n.s.v. 4 (16 August 1875), 195–6: https://biodiversitylibrary.org/page/33108754, and n.s.v.4 (21 August 1875), 226–7: https://biodiversitylibrary.org/page/33108785 [both accessed 2 October 2023].
10 Preston, Lancashire Archives, DRM/1/92, 1838.
11 Manchester, John Rylands Library, RYL/1/5/3, Index to Deeds and Documents, p. 156, plan by John S. Raby, June 1881, available online as 'Plan of Longford Park Estate', although with incorrect reference: https://luna.manchester.ac.uk/luna/servlet/detail/Manchester~91~1~112908~197978:Plan-of-Longford-Park-Estate?qvq=q%3Alongford&mi=1&trs=22 [accessed 2 October 2023]; Sale, Trafford Local Studies, STR/1/12/19/1 box 3 of 3, file 'Longford Park Purchase', 'Plan of Longford Hall Estate and Adjoining Properties belonging to Mr John Rylands'. Surveyed June 1881 [annotated] copy April 1885).
12 'Surveyor's report of buildings proposed to be retained (April 1911)', p. 2.
13 *Ibid.*, pp. 1–2.
14 *Ibid.*, pp. 2–3.
15 Sale, Trafford Local Studies, STR/1/2/2/8, Epitome of Proceedings, 21 June 1904, p. 76.
16 Surveyor's report, p. 2.
17 Sale, Trafford Local Studies, STR/1/2/2/1, Epitome of Proceedings, 24 May 1898, p. 444.
18 Surveyor's report, pp. 3–4.
19 *Ibid.*, pp. 4–5.
20 Sale, Trafford Local Studies, PLA/1/786/2–3, building plans, n.d.
21 Baines, 'Longford Hall', p. 227.
22 London, The National Archives, RG10/3971, f. 91, p. 56; the bothy is referenced in Appleby, 'Longford Hall', 417.
23 Surveyor's report, p. 3.
24 *Ibid.*, p. 1.
25 Farnie, 'John Rylands', 58–9.
26 E. Gow, 'Enriqueta Rylands: The Public and Private Collecting of a Nonconformist Bibliophile, 1889–1908' (PhD dissertation, The University of Manchester, 2023), p. 68: https://research.manchester.ac.uk/en/studentTheses/enriqueta-rylands-the-public-and-private-collecting-of-a-nonconfo [accessed 4 October 2023]; Sale, Trafford Local Studies, PLA/1/786/4–5, building plans, 1892.
27 Manchester, John Rylands Library, JRL/5/2/10a, plans of proposed alterations at Longford Hall, undated: https://luna.manchester.ac.uk/luna/servlet/s/0d5v60 [accessed 2 October 2023].
28 Manchester, John Rylands Library, ORF/3/1/36, Minute book of the Trustees of Mrs Rylands, 15 May 1908, p. 28.
29 Manchester, Manchester Archives, M10/1/5/60, Poor Rate Book, 11 July 1856, p. 6 entry 76; M10/1/5/61, Poor Rate Book, 7 July 1857, p. 3 entry 74.
30 *Manchester Guardian*, 7 February 1857, p. 2, col. 2.
31 Sale, Trafford Local Studies, STR/2/4/1, Poor Rate Book, 15 December 1858, p. 34 entry 858.

32 Manchester, Manchester Archives, M10/8/5/20, Poor Rate Book, 29 April 1858, p. 6 entry 69; M10/8/5/23, Poor Rate Book, April 1861, p. 6 entry 79.

33 Sale, Trafford Local Studies, STR/2/4/1, Poor Rate Book, 15 December 1858, p. 34 entry 858; STR/2/4/2, Poor Rate Book, 20 December 1860, p. 44 entry 1092; STR/2/4/3, Poor Rate Book, 16 August 1866, p. 60 entry 1417.

34 Farnie, 'John Rylands', 19.

35 Appleby, 'Longford Hall', 417.

36 R. Bond, 'The Family of the Radical Boroughreeve Thomas Walker (senior) of Longford', *Manchester Region History Review*, 1 (2022), 53–6: https://mcphh.files.wordpress.com/2022/06/mrhr_ns_1_bond.pdf [accessed 3 October 2023].

37 Manchester, Manchester Archives, M10/8/5/18, Poor Rate Book, 10 April 1856, p. 6 entry 74; M10/8/5/19, Poor Rate Book, April 1857, p. 6 entry 70.

38 Manchester, Manchester Archives, M10/8/5/20, Poor Rate Book, 29 April 1858, p. 6 entry 69.

39 Title deeds of owner of 68 Cromwell Road, in a private collection [loaned to the author in 2021].

40 B. T. Leech, *Old Stretford: Reminiscences of the Past Half Century* (Manchester City News, 1910), p. 22.

41 R. Bond, 'The Freehold Land Society Movement', *Manchester Group of the Victorian Society*, newsletter, Christmas 2022, 7–9: https://storage.victoriansociety.org.uk/source/Manchester%20newsletters/Christmas2022.pdf?_t=1669211909 [accessed 3 October 2023].

42 Manchester, John Rylands Library, RYL/1/5/3, Index to Deeds and Documents, p. 35.

43 Title deeds of owner of 68 Cromwell Road.

44 Appleby, 'Longford Hall', 418.

45 *Manchester Guardian*, 18 July 1855, p. 1, col. 5.

46 The Orford Papers, including residuary papers of Enriqueta Rylands, were donated to the John Rylands Library by the son of Lewis A. Orford, who had acted as solicitor to Enriqueta; Manchester, John Rylands Library, ORF/3/2/7, plan titled 'John Rylands Esqre Lodge Stretford', 28 March 1860.

47 Index to Deeds and Documents, pp. 17–18.

48 London, The National Archives, RG9/2865, f. 61, p. 19.

49 [Green], *In Memoriam*, p. 26.

50 H. T. Crofton, *A History of the Ancient Chapel of Stretford*, vol. III (Manchester: Chetham Society, 1903), p. 165

51 N. Pevsner, *Buildings of England: South Lancashire* (London: Penguin, 1969), p. 405; Farnie, 'John Rylands', 19.

52 Farnie, 'Enriqueta Augustina Rylands', 16.

53 C. Welch and L. E. Lauer, 'Samuel Gosnell Green', in Lawrence Goldman (ed.), *Oxford Dictionary of National Biography* (Oxford: Oxford University Press, 2004): https://doi.org/10.1093/ref:odnb/33534 [accessed 3 October 2023].

54 Farnie, 'John Rylands', pp. 31, 33.

55 Farnie, 'Enriqueta Augustina Rylands', 11–13; the 1861 census records Enriqueta Tennant in Lewisham: London, The National Archives, RG 9/413, f. 30, p. 17.

56 'Architecture and Art in Manchester', *The Builder*, 3 (1845), 546.
57 *Architects of Greater Manchester 1800–1940*: https://manchestervictorianarchitects.org.uk/index.php/architects/richard-lane [accessed 5 May 2024].
58 A. Kenney, 'Catalogue of the Archives of the Manchester Society of Architects', *Bulletin of the John Rylands University Library*, 74:2 (1992), 37–64.
59 *Architects of Greater Manchester*: https://manchestervictorianarchitects.org.uk/architects/philip-nunn [accessed 3 October 2023]; Kenney, 'Catalogue', 37–8.
60 Manchester, John Rylands Library, MSA/1/4/1, list of members, p. 4.
61 *Manchester Guardian*, 13 November 1866, p. 5, col. 5.
62 Manchester, John Rylands Library, MSA/1/2/3, report presented to the Annual Meeting, 24 June 1867, p. 8.
63 Manchester, John Rylands Library, MSA/1/2/4, report presented to the Annual Meeting, 22 June 1868, p. 3.
64 Ibid.
65 W. R. Corson, 'The views of Manchester architects', *The Builder*, 25 (1867), 850.
66 Manchester, Manchester Archives, M9/40/2/222, Poor Rate Book, 1859, p. 270 entry 1719; M9/40/2/264, Poor Rate Book, 1865, p. 287 entry 1225.
67 Manchester, Manchester Archives, M10/9/5/65, Poor Rate Book, 1867, p. 14 entry 5602.
68 London, Principal Probate Registry: https://probatesearch.service.gov.uk to [accessed 17 May 2024].
69 *Manchester Guardian*, 17 September 1867, p. 1, col. 2.
70 *Ibid.*, 24 August 1901, p. 8, col. 3.
71 Personal communication by email, 24 November 2022.
72 *Manchester Guardian*, 16 June 1858, p. 4, col. 4.
73 It should be noted that the online index to the *Manchester Guardian* can be somewhat haphazard, and articles were found in which Nunn's name appears, even rendered in capital letters, which were not found by a simple search for Nunn by name.
74 *Manchester Courier and Lancashire General Advertiser*, 11 September 1858, p. 12, col. 6 [accessed via the British Newspaper Archive (BNA)].
75 *Ibid.*, 8 May 1866, p. 1, col. 6; 14 April 1866, p. 8, col. 6; 12 May 1866, p. 8, col. 6 [all accessed via BNA].
76 *Manchester Guardian*, 6 August 1859, p. 7, col. 4.
77 *Ibid.*, 4 March 1865, p. 2, col. 5.
78 *Ibid.*, 20 August 1864, p. 2, col. 2.
79 *Architects of Greater Manchester*: https://manchestervictorianarchitects.org.uk/architects/philip-nunn [accessed 23 May 2024].
80 R. Bond, 'Plans by Philip Nunn, Architect', Manchester Group of *The Victorian Society*, newsletter (summer 2021), 13–15: https://storage.victoriansociety.org.uk/source/Manchester%20newsletters/ManchesterGroupNewsletterSummer2021.pdf [accessed 3 October 2023].
81 Manchester, Manchester Archives, Accession 2012/33, Elevations To New Streets, vol. 49. The plan is too fragile to access; see Bond, 'Plans by Philip Nunn', for a reproduction.

82 *Manchester Guardian*, 9 November 1859, p. 1, col. 2.
83 *Ibid.*, 12 August 1865, p. 2, col. 4.
84 Manchester, Manchester Archives, Accession 2012/33, Elevations To New Streets, vol. 49. The plan is too fragile to access; see Bond, 'Plans by Philip Nunn', for a reproduction.
85 *Manchester Guardian,* 26 September 1867, p. 1, col. 2.
86 Farnie, 'John Rylands', 19.
87 *Manchester Courier and Lancashire General Advertiser*, 20 July 1865, p. 1 [accessed via BNA]; M. Nevell, 'Nico Ditch: Investigating an Early Medieval Monument, 1883–2023', *Transactions of the Lancashire and Cheshire Antiquarian Society*, 114 (2023), 217–8.
88 *Manchester Guardian*, 26 December 1871, p. 2, col. 4, is the earliest advert.
89 London, The National Archives, RG 11/3888, f. 19, p. 32.
90 Manchester Guardian, 15 September 1879, p. 8, col. 4.
91 J. Parker, 'John Rylands', *Daily News*, 7 October 1889, p. 8.
92 Manchester, John Rylands Library, Douglas Farnie Papers, DFP box 2/5), file 're. 1994 inquiry and Longford Hall demolition', English Heritage statement, 1994, p. 2.
93 F. Salmon, 'The Battle of the Styles Continued?', *The Victorian Society in Manchester*, newsletter (summer 2014), p. 2.
94 C. Stewart, *The Stones of Manchester* (London: Edward Arnold, 1956), pp. 33–5, 38.
95 'An Architectural Address in Manchester', *The Builder*, 34 (1876), 16.
96 H.-R. Hitchcock, *Architecture: Nineteenth and Twentieth Centuries* (Harmondsworth: Penguin, 1977), pp. 328–9.
97 Bond, 'Plans by Philip Nunn', 13–14.
98 Hitchcock, *Architecture*, p. 354.
99 Farnie, 'John Rylands', 37.
100 Pevsner, *Buildings of England*, p. 405; Manchester, John Rylands Library, Douglas Farnie Papers, DFP box 2/5, English Heritage Statement, 1994, p. 2.
101 Manchester, John Rylands Library, Douglas Farnie Papers, DFP box 2/5, English Heritage statement, p. 2.
102 *Ibid*.
103 *Ibid.*, p. 3.
104 *Ibid*.
105 Manchester, John Rylands Library, Douglas Farnie Papers, DFP box 2/5, M. Lowe, 'Longford Hall Inquiry Closing Submissions for Trafford MBC', 13 May 1994, p. 13.
106 Manchester, John Rylands Library, Douglas Farnie Papers, DFP box 2/5, letter from Douglas Farnie, 27 July 1993.
107 Manchester, John Rylands Library, Douglas Farnie Papers, DFP box 2/5, 'Proof of Evidence in Relation to John Rylands of Longford Hall', 5 April 1994.
108 Cambridge, Cambridge University Library, Planning Reports, Trafford Metropolitan Borough Council; 'Longford Hall, 1994', GBR/3296/Maps/Maps.PL.02.Trafford, 1994:1b; 'The Architectural and Historical Interest of Longford Hall', pp. 1–20: https://archivesearch.lib.cam.ac.uk/repositories/2/archival_objects/260283 [accessed 4 October 2023].

109 *Ibid.*, p. 8.
110 Manchester, John Rylands Library, Douglas Farnie Papers, DFP box 2/5, 'John Rylands of Longford Hall: A Comment Upon the Report by Mr. J. Ayers with particular reference to the three pages (pp. 6-9) relating to John Rylands', 29 June 1992.
111 *Ibid.*, pp. 16-19.
112 *Ibid.*, pp. 6-8; C. W. Sutton, 'John Rylands (1801-1888)', in L. Stephen and S. Lee (eds), *Dictionary of National Biography* (London: Smith, Elder, and Co., 1885-1900): https://doi.org/10.1093/odnb/9780192683120.013.24416 [accessed 21 May 2024]; D. A. Farnie, 'John Rylands of Manchester', *Bulletin of the John Rylands Library*, 56:1 (1973), 93-129.
113 Manchester, John Rylands Library, Douglas Farnie Papers, DFP 2/5, Lowe, p. 12.
114 Farnie, 'Wiener Thesis', p. 86.
115 Gow 'Enriqueta Rylands', p. 68.
116 Farnie, 'Enriqueta Augustina Rylands', 3-38.
117 Gow, 'Enriqueta Rylands', p. 68.
118 Sale, Trafford Local Studies, PLA/1/786/5, building plan, 1892.
119 D. Brady, 'The New Longford Estate, Stretford' (published privately).

The English Gift after the Destruction of the University of Louvain Library in World War I

CATHLEEN HOENIGER, QUEEN'S UNIVERSITY, CANADA

Abstract

The deliberate destruction of the university library in Louvain during World War I caused an international outcry, but also elicited constructive reactions. One of the most impressive responses was the collection in England of an enormous donation of books to replace those lost, a project coordinated by the John Rylands Library in Manchester. Although the librarian, Henry Guppy, documented the donation in issues of the *Bulletin of the John Rylands Library*, this generous and altruistic work has received little mention in the recent scholarship on the burning of the library and its rebuilding. This article charts the development of the project and the extent of the contribution, drawing on Guppy's publications and documents in the library archives of the University of Manchester, Oxford University and the University of Toronto. Some of the most valuable gifts from private individuals receive special attention, as do the institutional donations by the Bodleian Library and the University of Toronto.

Keywords: University of Louvain Library; John Rylands Library; biblioclasm; World War I; rare books; incunables; Henry Guppy; Bodleian Library; University of Toronto Library

Close to the beginning of World War I, the event that created more alarm than almost any other was the unbridled attack on Louvain in Belgium. Historic and cultural sites were targeted, and the university library was completely destroyed. The attack in the final week of August 1914 was part of widespread reprisals by German army divisions, after their progress across neutral Belgium towards France was hampered by Belgian forces. Although some historic centres were treated with respect, a remarkable situation in Louvain – in which Germans soldiers in confusion fired on their own comrades – provoked extreme anger against the local people. During five terrible days, close to two hundred civilians were killed, about 650 were taken captive, and over a thousand private homes and historic buildings were ruined, among them the fifteenth-century church of Saint-Pierre.[1]

On the evening of 25 August, the houses surrounding the Old Market Square were systematically destroyed by German soldiers using small explosives and incendiary pastilles. At about 11.30 p.m., the University Hall, which occupied most of a city block on Naamsestraat, had its doors broken down and a devastating fire was lit. The building was a medieval cloth hall that had been enlarged in stages. By 1690, the renovated upper storey held the library, but a new wing was built for the books between 1723 and 1733. When the hall went up in flames, the entire library, including close to one thousand manuscripts and about 800 incunables, was lost in a blaze that lasted ten hours. From the ruins, only some burned and compressed volumes and fragments of vellum manuscripts could be recovered.[2] A few of these telling tomes were later encased in glass frames and placed on display in the new university library.[3] Several fragments from a manuscript were made into a memento for Henry Guppy, the librarian of the John Rylands Library in Manchester, in thanks for his work in the aftermath of the tragedy to assemble a collection of books for the revitalisation of the University of Louvain Library (Figure 1).

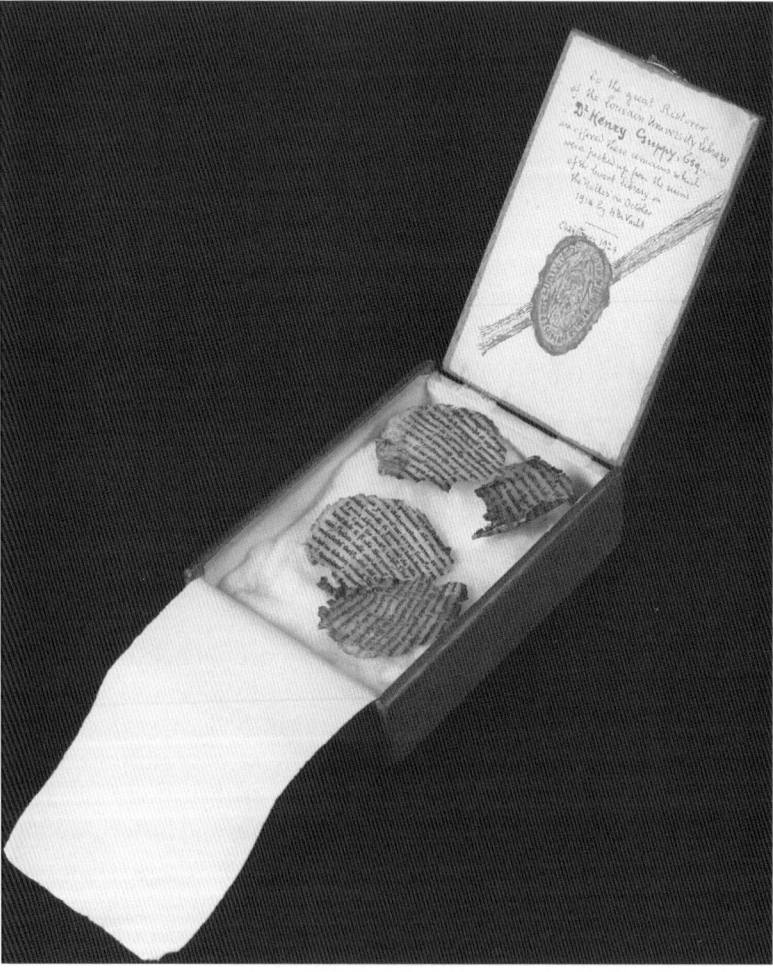

Figure 1 Memento for Henry Guppy, Fragments from Louvain Library, Latin MS 447, Rylands Collection, The University of Manchester Library. Image copyright © The University of Manchester.

The idea of an English book donation took root in December 1914, at the initiative of the governors and librarian of the John Rylands Library. A year later, in London, a committee was set up by the British Academy and sanctioned by the British Parliament to offer support to Louvain, and by December 1916 the British Academy committee was working in full cooperation with the Rylands in Manchester, where the collecting of books was already well under way.[4] The project spearheaded in Manchester was remarkable because, in contrast to the flood of angry outpourings against Germany in the press, feelings of sympathy were given substance through a donation that ultimately amounted to 55,782 volumes. Before this investigation turns to focus on the English gift, the reason why the loss of the university library in Louvain occasioned so much distress should be explained.

The University of Louvain was internationally famous because it had the earliest foundation of any university in the Low Countries, begun as a *studium generale* with the issue of a papal bull from Pope Martin V in 1425. A number of world-renowned scholars were associated with the university, most notably Desiderius Erasmus, Andreas Vesalius and Gerardus Mercator.[5] The 'old' university had a famous central library by the seventeenth century, which represented the unification of many earlier, separate collegiate collections and the libraries of professors, as well as substantial legacies donated from the early 1600s.[6] During the eighteenth century, the library grew much larger still, among other things via the acquisition of the library of the Jesuit Order in Louvain after its suppression in 1773.[7] However, two decades later, the tumultuous events in the Low Countries that directly followed the French Revolution resulted in the closure of the University of Louvain and the dispersal of much of its library. In 1795, French commissioners, one of whom was the director of the Bibliothèque Mazarine of the University of Paris, removed to Paris over a thousand of the most precious volumes, where they have remained since.[8] After the Austrian Netherlands was ceded to France in 1797, about 700 volumes from the remaining collection were taken for the new École Centrale in Brussels, and these eventually became part of the Royal Library of Belgium. Later, in the wake of Napoleon's fall, a state university was opened in Louvain, but then, in 1835, the institution took on its religious identity as the Katholieke Universiteit Leuven (KU Leuven). After 1835, the library that had been closed and pillaged by the French was built up again.[9]

Therefore, the library destroyed in August 1914 was not the fabled collection associated with the early university and its remarkable scholars. Nevertheless, the modern library comprised about 300,000 printed volumes and over a thousand manuscripts and incunables. As Richard Ovenden has explained, the library was of great artistic, intellectual, and cultural value: 'the importance of the library could be seen in its glorious baroque buildings. Its holdings reflected Belgian cultural identity, documenting the intellectual contribution of the greatest minds of the region, and preserving the university's strongly Catholic cultural flavour. It was also a national resource, as a library of legal deposit and open to the general public.'[10]

A full assessment of the quality of the library that was lost, however, is almost impossible. The new librarian, Paul Delannoy, had just begun to make a proper inventory of the holdings in 1912. There were manuscripts from the Near and Middle East, and collections of oriental books that had never been catalogued.[11] It is also important to correct one persistent mistake about the treasures that perished in the fire, which concerns a printing on vellum of Andreas Vesalius's *De humani corporis fabrica libri septem* (Basel: Oporinus, 1543), supposedly created for Emperor Charles V. As Omer Steeno and Maurits Biesbrouck, two historians of medicine from Leuven, contend, it is unlikely that the *De fabrica* was ever printed on vellum because of its very large size. Steeno and Biesbrouck also point out that the presentation volume for Charles V has survived in a French private collection, and suggest that the copy that was lost in 1914 was probably the one bequeathed by Georges d'Autriche, Chancellor of Louvain and Dean of Saint-Pierre, in 1619.[12]

This study of the English donation has benefited from considerable scholarship on the University of Louvain Library, in which various approaches have been pursued. Intensive interest has been shown in the destruction of the library in relation to the events of World War I in Belgium, and the complicated local history of Louvain (Leuven).[13] The attack on the library has also been considered from a broad, comparative perspective as one example among many in the long history of targeting libraries during military conflicts.[14] Such displays of force against centres of learning did not serve strategic military purposes, but rather were used as an insidious way of breaking resistance by demoralising civilian populations. In 1992, the destruction of Sarajevo's National Library during the four-year siege of the city by the Serbs spurred on further study of biblioclasm in association with wars and ethnic cleansing.[15] More recently, as the centenaries of the beginning and end of World War I have come and gone, the University of Louvain Library has been featured in commemorative conferences and exhibitions.[16] Scholars affiliated with the KU Leuven have carried out detailed research on the German occupation, and taken on the challenge of integrating information from eye-witness accounts into a more abstracted analysis.[17]

Returning to the final days in August 1914, the library's deliberate destruction created shock waves outside Belgium due to reverence for the historic university. Within days of the fire, the international press had captured the dismay and anger of continental, British, and American politicians, intellectuals, and concerned citizens.[18] Scholars have investigated how news outlets in allied and neutral countries covered the incident, including the opportunistic appearance of strongly anti-German cartoons in British and American publications.[19]

Regarding the more constructive and far-sighted gestures, most recognition has been given to the American gift of a new library building for Louvain. The library was designed by the American architect, Whitney Warren, to resemble a Flemish seventeenth-century hall, but on a larger scale to allow sufficient space for up to two million books. Warren also selected the new building site, in a prominent location on the Volksplein (or Place du Peuple), where an entire block of houses had been destroyed.[20] To fund the new library, $500,000 was raised in the first campaign, begun in October 1919 and chaired by the peace activist and president of Columbia University, Nicholas Murray Butler. In 1925, however, with the library only half-built, funds ran out, and a new campaign had to be launched. Concerned that the image of American philanthropy might be tarnished by the unfinished library, John D. Rockefeller Jr, who had already aided France in the restoration of Reims Cathedral, led the way with a contribution of $100,000.[21] However, $550,000 more had to be raised in the United States to finish the building. Unfortunately, the new library building later came to be associated with the stigmatisation of the Germans as barbaric owing to plans for an inscription on the balustrade of the facade about the German propensity for violence, even though the inscription was never installed.[22]

In contrast, little has been written about many other helpful reactions to the loss of the library from institutions and individuals in several other countries. More than twenty committees were established on the continent, in the United Kingdom, and in the United States to solicit funds, donate food, and gather books. The first constructive responses came from the Netherlands and France very soon after the fire had taken its toll.[23] Among the British reactions, the director of Oxford University Press funnelled profits from the publication of *Why We Are at War: Britain's Case* into the Belgian Relief Fund.[24] Not only were these demonstrations of solidarity overshadowed at the time by the ostentatious American gift of the new library building, but they have also failed to garner much attention in the subsequent literature.

When, much later, Henry Guppy of the John Rylands Library recapitulated the growth of the 'scheme' to assist the University of Louvain Library, he described the American donation of the library building as having emerged in cooperation with the English gift of books. Guppy explained that, as a result of the appeals launched in Britain in 1915–16, the Americans had expressed their desire to collaborate.[25] Because the United States maintained neutrality for most of World War I, however, their overt participation in the project began only after the war had ended, and then took the form of an 'offer to rebuild the library'.[26] Yet when a celebration was held in Louvain for the laying of the library's foundation stone, on 28 July 1921, the small contingent of English representatives had to sit on the sidelines. From Britain, Guppy attended together with the Chairman of the Governors of the John Rylands Library, the Master of Christ's College, Cambridge, and Bodley's librarian, Dr Arthur E. Cowley. In the pages of the *Bulletin of the John Rylands Library*, Guppy recounted what had been evident to all those present: 'this was America's day. It was to America primarily that the gratitude of the University and of the people turned.'[27] Guppy could not help but add, however, that, on this occasion, 'the representatives of the English Committee … [had] recalled to mind with pardonable pride that it was in England that this movement began.'[28]

Since the remarkable and altruistic initiative of the John Rylands Library has not been fully acknowledged by scholars, it is the purpose of this article to recall to mind the English book project.[29] At the time, Guppy published many reports in the *Bulletin of the John Rylands Library* on the initiative, and in the first years he listed the gifts of books and their donors. With Guppy as the 'prime mover', over 55,000 volumes were amassed.[30] In recognition, the University of Louvain conferred upon

Guppy an honorary doctorate, and still in 1925, Guppy was receiving personal expressions of thanks from the rector and professors at Louvain.[31] In broaching this topic, the first step is to situate the idea hatched at the John Rylands Library in Manchester in relation to other British reactions within academic circles and government to the burning of the library. A second goal is to explore how the book project blossomed into a national and international enterprise. To suggest the breadth and depth of the English gift, this article considers some of the rare books and the individuals who donated them. Two substantial but very different donations from university libraries – the Bodleian Library in Oxford and the University of Toronto Library – receive attention. Nevertheless, it is essential to remember the very unfortunate loss of almost all of the volumes that comprised the English gift when the University of Louvain's new library was shelled and caught fire during World War II. Only about fifty quarto volumes, less than one-thousandth of the English donation, were recorded as having survived the second fire.[32] For this reason, when specific rare books that were part of the English donation to Louvain are considered in this article, volumes from the same printings that are housed today in different libraries are featured in place of the now-lost tomes.

At the outset, it is worth considering the immediate reaction in Britain to the burning of the library, as recorded in Britain's leading newspaper, *The Times*. This is especially true, given that some of the early letters printed reflected the views of educated individuals and university professors who fully understood the value of an excellent university library. Beginning three days after the fire, *The Times* featured Louvain in headlined articles, editorials, quotations from political speeches, and letters to the editor. The initial opinion pieces, presumably written by senior editorial staff, were inflammatory. The Germans were condemned for returning to the barbarism of the 'Dark Ages' in headlines that read 'Louvain in Ashes. Terrible Act of German Vandalism', and 'The March of the Huns', while the Kaiser was branded 'the modern Atilla'.[33] By the following week, however, some of the letters to the editor included more reflective statements on the significance of the destruction as a criminal act, and on what form of punishment would be appropriate.[34]

The London jurist, Frederick Pollock, recommended a 'judicial and dispassionate' reaction to the destruction.[35] Pollock was alluding to the recently codified, international laws of war – the Hague Convention of 1907 – of which Germany was one of forty-two signatories alongside Belgium, France, and the United Kingdom. Article 27 of the convention stipulated that buildings used for religion, art, science, and charity, hospitals, and historic monuments be spared unless they were being used for military purposes.[36] Arthur Evans, Chair of Archaeology at Oxford and President of the Society of Antiquaries, whose name was familiar because of his discovery of the ruins of the Bronze Age city of Knossos in Crete, used potent language to evoke the horror, and even sinfulness, of the destruction. He employed the term 'holocaust' – in the Ancient Greek sense, metaphorically comparing the burning of Louvain to a ritual of animal sacrifice – three times.[37] Evans also offered his opinion on the retribution the Germans should have to pay for breaking the rules of the Hague Convention, anticipating by several years one article of the Treaty of

Versailles when he suggested that German art museums should return paintings by Flemish masters, such as Dieric Bouts's *Altarpiece of the Holy Sacrament* (1464–68) – originally commissioned for the church of Saint-Pierre in Louvain – and that German libraries should 'more than make good the losses of Louvain'.[38] Consequently, close to the beginning of World War I, the destruction of the University of Louvain Library occasioned prescient evaluations by noted legal and academic individuals, which were widely circulated in *The Times*, concerning the application of the international laws of war to the assessment of the German action.

By Tuesday, 2 September 1914, collective reactions from academic institutions in the British Isles were beginning to be reported in *The Times*. In a statement from the National University of Ireland, the German act of biblioclasm was associated with the legendary destruction of the ancient *Mouseion* or library of Alexandria. Expressing the recognition that 'ignorance in arms' had often been responsible for the extinction of 'the records and achievements of civilization', the Irish university voiced their appeal to 'the universities of all nations to unite in a protest against an act so disastrous to the progress of mankind'.[39] In other words, a call was put out for academic solidarity at an international level against the German destruction and in sympathy with the university community in Louvain.

Although the John Rylands Library was, at the time, a city library rather than a university library, it was in solidarity with other libraries that the constructive and generous gesture took root in Manchester. As Guppy related in the *Bulletin*, the library's governing council had decided in December 1914 that their 'deep feelings of sympathy' should be given 'some practical expression ... [in] the form of a gift of books'.[40] Indeed, among the institutions of learning that responded to the plight of Louvain, the John Rylands Library, a richly endowed public library, was one of the first to move beyond words to assistance of a substantial nature. At first, the objective was to select donations from among the duplicates in the library, as well as to give copies of books the library had published – among them, catalogues of the collection, records of special exhibitions, and facsimiles of particularly valuable volumes in the library. This initial gift comprised about two hundred volumes. Soon after, an appeal was extended to readers of the *Bulletin* for donations.[41] By the summer of 1917, a wider call for donations was issued 'through the Press' at the instigation of Lord Muir Mackenzie, who chaired the committee established under the auspices of the British Academy in London.[42] As mentioned, the British government had supported the creation of a separate committee and book collection project in London and, initially, Hugh Butler, librarian of the House of Lords, was appointed to handle donations at the London end. By December 1916, however, the London committee began to cooperate fully with the John Rylands Library, and ultimately the coordination of all the donations fell to Guppy.[43]

The response to these appeals was enormous, and over a period of eleven years from 1915 to 1926, gifts of books flooded in from all over the United Kingdom and from many donors overseas. It was a laborious undertaking that required copious correspondence with donors to encourage gifts but also to avoid duplication and arrange shipping. The large majority of the work was taken on by Guppy, despite the depleted complement of library staff during the war years owing to military service.[44] Guppy showed an exceptional commitment to the enterprise, as evidenced by his timely responses to potential donors. Once the John Rylands Library became the British depository for all the book donations destined for Louvain, thousands of volumes had to be examined and prepared for sending.[45]

Because this article focuses on an exceptionally large and generous donation of books to revitalise a lost library, it seems appropriate to emphasise that the library where the project began had very recent origins, and was itself the result of an extraordinary gift. It was less than fifteen years before the tragedy in Belgium that the John Rylands Library had welcomed its first readers. Therefore, when Louvain's renowned library fell victim amidst war, those at the John Rylands Library could appreciate the magnitude of the loss for the university, the town, and the wider community.

The John Rylands Library was the gift of Enriqueta Augustina Rylands, in honour of her late husband, the wealthy cotton manufacturer and philanthropist John Rylands.[46] Enriqueta Rylands financed and supervised the building of the magnificent library, designed by Basil Champneys in a Victorian, neo-gothic style, and she furnished the library with an extraordinary collection of manuscripts and books – the result of two astounding purchases. In 1892, for about £250,000, Enriqueta bought the Althorp Library, property of the fifth Earl Spencer (John Poyntz Spencer, also known as Viscount Althorp), which comprised about 40,000 volumes and was described as the 'most beautiful and richest private library in Europe'.[47] The strengths of Althorp's collection lay in early humanist editions of Ancient Greek and Latin authors, particularly from the Venetian press of Aldus Manutius, as well as many examples from the cradle of English printing, most notably from the press of William Caxton. After the Althorp purchase, Enriqueta hired as librarian the Oxford graduate Edward Gordon Duff (1863–1924), an outstanding bibliographer who specialised in early English printing and stamped bindings.[48] Then, in 1901, Enriqueta bought an enormous collection of papyri, manuscripts, and rare Chinese and Japanese books, which had formed part of the library of the 25th and 26th earls of Crawford (Alexander Lindsay, 1812–80, and his son James Ludovic Lindsay, 1847–1913), known as the *Bibliotheca Lindesiana*.[49] Primarily rich in Middle Eastern and Asian materials, the Crawford purchase also encompassed some Western manuscripts, such as a fourteenth-century Italian codex of verses by Dante and Petrarch, with decorated borders featuring portraits of the poets and their ladies.[50]

At first, Enriqueta kept most of the Crawford collection with her at Longford Hall, but upon her death in 1908, all the manuscripts and books came as part of her estate to the John Rylands Library. Formally inaugurated on 6 October 1899, the doors of the John Rylands Library were opened to the public on 1 January 1900. A few months earlier, in June 1899, Henry Guppy was appointed joint librarian together with Duff. After Duff had chaperoned the collection from the Rylands's estate to the new library, however, he resigned in October 1900 and Guppy became librarian, in which capacity he served until his death in 1948.[51]

Guppy took on the principal responsibility for the book donations to Louvain, from December 1914 until 1926. The initial, circumscribed gift of almost two hundred volumes was welcomed by Albert Carnoy, Professor of Classics and Linguistics at Louvain, who acknowledged that this gesture represented one of the 'very first' attempts to resurrect their library.[52] Soon after, Guppy recorded his realisation that other institutions or individuals might wish to be part of the project, and announced that the library would coordinate these donations, and a careful register of the donors and their contributions would be assembled to be given to the University of Louvain together with the books.[53]

To encourage book donations that were appropriate, Guppy was careful to circulate information on the nature of the holdings that had been lost. At the outset, the *Bulletin* featured an article by Léon van der Essen, Professor of History at Louvain, in which he sketched the characteristics of the destroyed collection.[54] Like many university libraries in Europe, the principal strengths had been in classics and theology. Louvain was a Catholic university, and had been a centre of theological discussion and debate for centuries. The holdings, of course, reflected what was taught and studied, including the beliefs of the religious communities in Louvain, among them prominent Jesuits and exponents of Jansenism. The tragic loss of the manuscripts and incunables also received emphasis in the *Bulletin* and the press.

Since most of the donors to the Manchester initiative were English speaking, a sizeable percentage of the books that were assembled had naturally been written in English and published in Great Britain (although there were numerous exceptions, as will be explained). In subject matter, the gifts generally represented the traditions of university learning in Britain, which similarly gave primacy to classics and theology, but also encompassed history, literature, and the sciences. Some donors, however, who had substantial libraries from which to select their gifts, thoughtfully sought to tie their donations to Louvain's specific needs. This was manifest in books that were written in French and German, in treatises on subjects of particular relevance to Louvain and, occasionally, in an attempt to replace the more valuable books that had been lost. Several donors gave French or German books, some of which were also early printings. Frank Falkner of Bowdon in Cheshire, for example, donated an important early book in French on traditional customary law in Normandy, published in Caen in 1510.[55] Out of nineteen books dating from the eighteenth to the early twentieth century that were the gift of R. L. Kenyon of Oswestry in Shropshire, eighteen were in French.[56]

Numerous theological books were donated, and in several instances the gifts reflected a sensitivity to the former strength of the University of Louvain Library in early printings. Mr John Laird Busk and his wife Eleanor Joy Busk of Westerham in Kent gave religious books from the first decades of printing in Germany: a German edition of Cassianus's treatise on the Desert Fathers, published in Augsburg in 1472; one of Martin Luther's sermons, published in Augsburg c.1520; and three German bibles from the 1520s–30s.[57] Other donors chose to give religious treatises directly associated with Louvain and its theologians. For instance, the Manchester booksellers, Messrs Sherratt and Hughes, contributed eleven books by the Flemish Jesuit priest Cornelius Lapide (who had studied theology at Louvain), which had been published in Antwerp between 1694 and 1705.[58] More than twenty Jesuitical treatises were given by Sir Ernest Mason Satow (1843–1929) of Ottery St Mary, a British diplomat stationed for many years in Japan. Some of these were writings by Ignatius of Loyola, several of which were published in Antwerp in the seventeenth century.[59] Two more donors sought to match their gifts to the Catholic history of the institution: Walter J. Kaye of Harrogate gave three theological treatises that had been printed in Louvain in the seventeenth century, and Kenneth F. Gibbs, Archdeacon of St Albans, donated two treatises on Antwerp written by the Jesuit Carolus Scribanius and issued by the famous Plantin Press in Antwerp in 1610.[60]

Donors also contributed volumes that recalled the breadth of learning at the early university, which, apart from theology, encompassed aspects of the humanities and the sciences. At the core of the *studia humanitatis* in the Renaissance was the interpretation of celebrated Ancient Greek and Latin authors, and a few of the donations reflected the sophistication of leading scholars of Ancient Greek in the first half of the sixteenth century. One gift, from Mrs M. E. Gray of Chester, was the second humanist edition of Pindar's victory or 'epinician' odes, celebrating athletic victory at the Panhellenic competitions.[61] Published in Rome in 1515, two years after the first printing by Aldus Manutius, the Roman version was based on a different collection of manuscripts and included the abundant Greek *scholia* or commentary on these verses. Staffan Fogelmark has described the *editio Romana* as 'the most important Pindar edition ever', because it 'became the vulgate text for three hundred years'.[62] The first Greek press in Rome was set up by Zacharias Kallierges, with the financial and intellectual support of the humanist Cornelio Benigo, in the 'house' of the enormously wealthy banker Agostino Chigi, later called the Villa Farnesina.[63] The title page of the Pindar featured the emblematic devices of Benigo and Kallierges, printed side by side: for Benigo, a caduceus topped by wings and a star, and for Kallierges – who hailed from a Cretan family with imperial lineage – a double-headed eagle.[64] Although quite plain, red ink was used to colour the historiated initial and the first lines of text for the Olympian and Pythian odes (Figure 2). The 1515 volume was printed in a relatively small Greek font, with Pindar's verses arranged in a block at the upper left or upper right on each page, and the ancient *scholia* configured around the poetry.

Another early printing in Greek was the 1532 (or second edition) of the speeches of Demosthenes of Athens (*c*.384–22 BC). Aldus Manutius had issued the *editio princeps* in 1504, but this new folio was published by Johannes Hervagius in Basel.[65] Hervagius, who worked at the Swiss press of Johann Froben until Froben's death in 1527, subsequently established his own printing house for ancient and theological works. Although indebted to the Aldine printing, the 1532 Demosthenes was an ambitious endeavour. With the scholar Johannes Oporinus as editor, this volume of more than five hundred pages opened with a short preface in Latin by Erasmus, and continued with extracts from ancient writers on Demosthenes, the complete text of his speeches in Greek, and *scholia* on the speeches. For the first time,

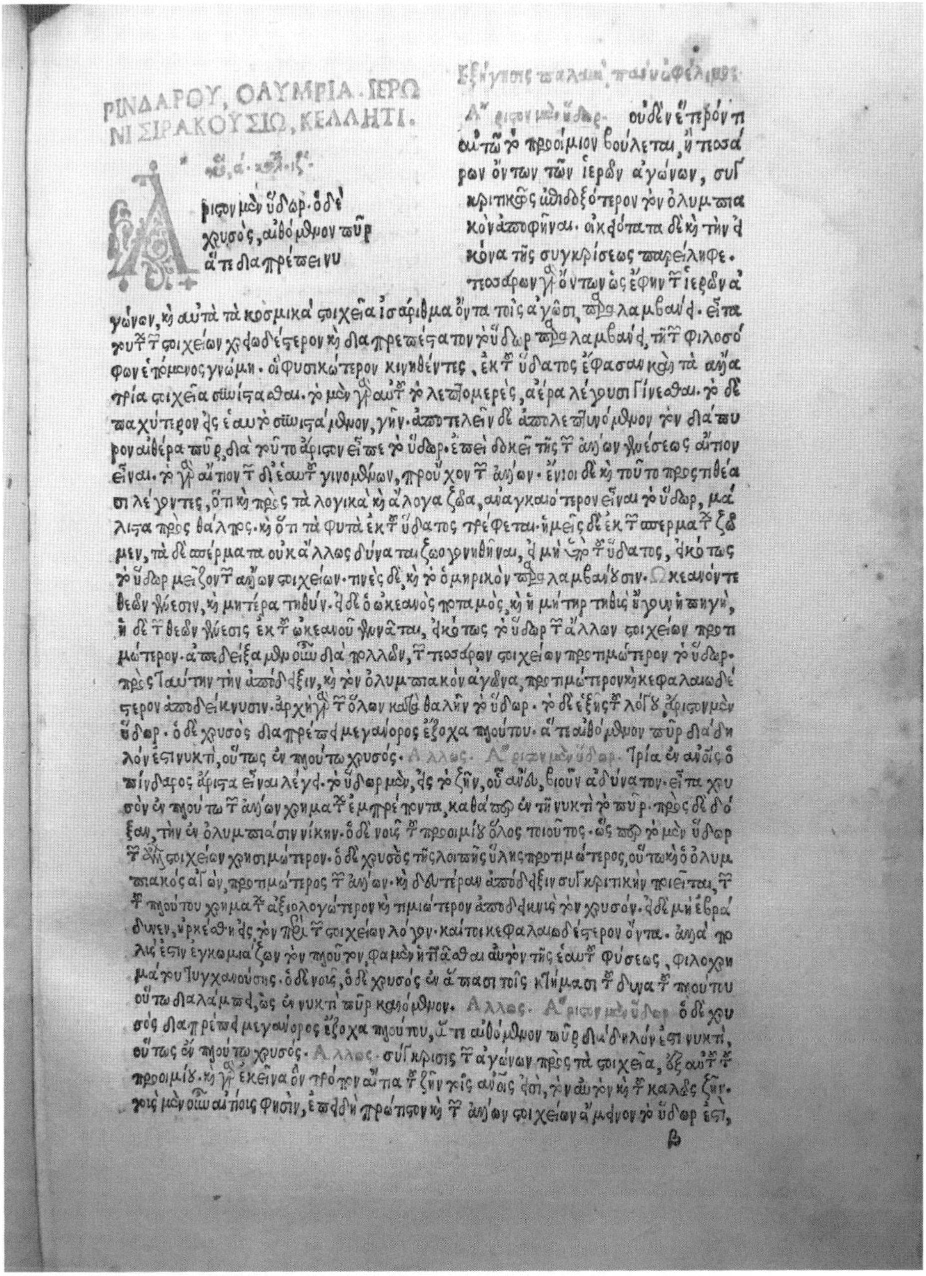

Figure 2 Pindar, *Olympian, Pythian, Nemean and Isthmian Odes*, in Greek (Rome: Zacharias Kallierges, 1515), first page of Olympian Odes with scholia. Thomas Fisher Rare Book Library, University of Toronto, D-10/00464.

Renaissance commentary was included as an addendum of fifty pages.[66] The complexity of this production can be seen from the fact that many of the pages had to be set up for printing in two stages, with a central box on the page for Demosthenes's oration in Greek type, and the *scholia* arranged around it in a smaller, more tightly spaced Greek font. Hervagius's elaborate device appears on the title page and the final leaf, comprised of a bust-length statue of a three-headed Hermes (*Hermes Trikephalos*) on top of a column, from which a lion's head was suspended.[67] Attractive woodcuts were employed for the historiated initials to mark the beginning of each section, with the most elaborate one showing a courtly scene with a king looking down from his castle at a lady and two lovers in a garden (Figure 3).

Since Cicero, Demosthenes had been known for the eloquence of his writing style, but in the Renaissance, the content of his orations was also valued, since he had used forceful rhetoric to argue that Athens must hold strong against her enemies.[68] During World War I, however, the gift of this book to Louvain may have seemed appropriate because Erasmus of Rotterdam, who had taught briefly at Louvain, strongly promoted the study of Demosthenes.[69] The volume was donated by J. G. Milne, who had studied classics at Oxford.[70] But as his books were being packed to send to Manchester, Milne noticed that several were in bad condition, and expressing to Guppy his desire that they 'go in a decent state to their new abode', he offered to cover the cost of their rebinding.[71]

In addition to donations that complemented the association of famous humanists with Louvain, several gifts paid tribute to the pursuit of the mathematical sciences during the early modern period in the Low Countries. Among a generous list from Aberdeen University Library was the first edition of an astronomical treatise by the Dutch mathematician and instrument maker, Christiaan Huygens, the *Systema Saturnium* (The Hague: Adriaan Vlacq, 1659). In this book, Huygens described the appearance of Saturn with one of its moons and the ring surrounding the planet, recording his observations using the first powerful Keplerian telescope, which he and his brother Constantijn had made.[72] Considered one of the most important publications in the history of western science, another first edition sold at auction in the United States in 2010 for $30,000.[73]

Turning to the mapping of the earth rather than the heavens, included in a large gift by the family of the late Sir Charles Nicholson was a treatise on the Holy Land, *Theatrum Terrae Sanctae*, by the Catholic priest from Delft, Christiaan van Adrichem (1533–85). The copy given was a first edition, published by Georg Braun in Cologne in 1590, after Van Adrichem had fled religious persecution in the Low Countries and taken refuge in the German lands.[74] In the text, Van Adrichem ranged widely in a manner typical of the day, beginning with descriptions of the geography of ancient Palestine and the treasures of Jerusalem, including a catalogue of numerous places significant to the twelve tribes of Israel, such as Bethlehem and the Dead Sea, and charting the long history of the region through the rule of emperors and popes.

Although the treatise remains of interest to historians of the Reformation and Counter-Reformation, the book is treasured primarily for its engraved maps.

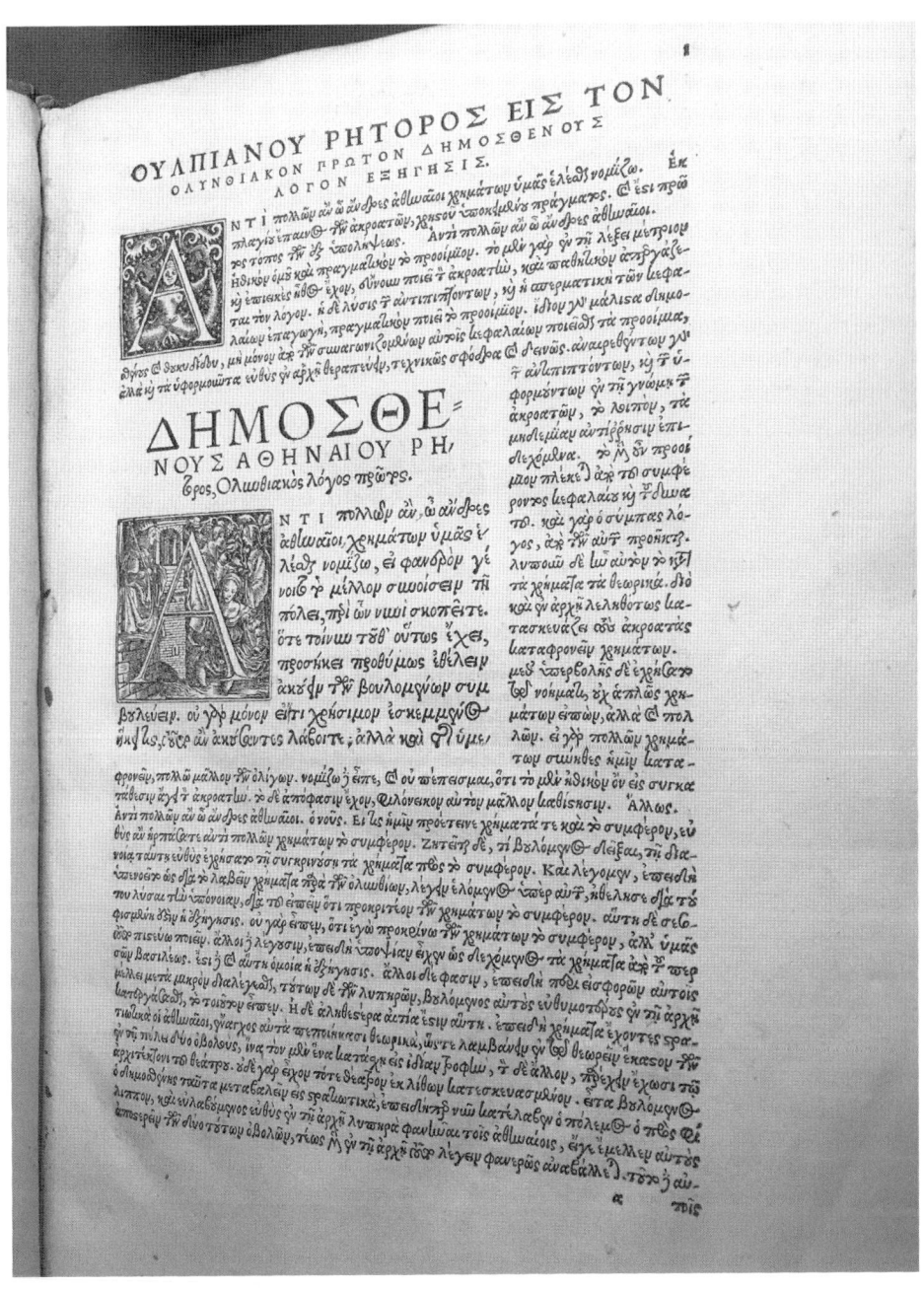

Figure 3 Demosthenes, *Orations*, in Greek (Basel: Johannes Hervagius, 1532), Decorated initials for the letter 'A' on page with Demosthenes' oration and scholia. Thomas Fisher Rare Book Library, University of Toronto, E-10/00711.

Van Adrichem had never actually travelled to the Near East, but as a result of his training as a surveyor, and his intensive study of literary accounts and earlier cartography, he was able to fix events from sacred history in the geographical space of his maps. The book opens with a large, fold-out depiction of the entire Holy Land (*Situs Terrae Promissionis SS Bibliorum*) and, as the treatise progresses, ten smaller, inserted maps chart the lands once inhabited by the twelve Hebrew tribes. Most spectacular is the fold-out plan of Jerusalem at the end of the volume, representing the city during Christ's lifetime.[75] Kenneth Nebenzahl, a historian of cartography, described this bird's-eye view of Jerusalem as 'the most dramatic and important of the 16th century', and stressed the remarkable degree of its accuracy.[76] Labels on the city plan allowed readers to find sacred monuments and trace significant journeys that were mentioned in the text. From the palace of Pontius Pilate in the centre left of the plan, one could follow Jesus on the road to Calvary, outside the city walls at the bottom left. The fourteen Stations of the Cross were depicted, allowing viewers to link Christ's tragic journey to sites on the map of the Holy City, so as to secure the events in their visual memory. For students at the University of Louvain in the 1920s and 1930s, these detailed maps with representations of emblematic locations and monuments illustrated how much was known in the sixteenth century about this potently religious but chronically contested part of the world.

Indeed, in their collective desire to revitalise the University of Louvain Library, it is clear that many British donors sought to tailor their gifts to the needs of the Belgian students. A. T. Porter of Chelsea in London, for example, gave a folio volume with a treatise by the Dutch legal scholar, Hugo Grotius, on the struggle for independence from Spanish rule in the Netherlands during the late sixteenth century, *Annales et Historiae de Rebus Belgicis* (first edn, Amsterdam: Joannis Blaeu, 1657).[77] In a similar spirit, John Grant of Edinburgh donated Jean de Beaurain's *Histoire de la Campagne de 1674 en Flandres* (Paris: Jombert, Delaguette et Monory, 1774), which was a folio of considerable value, and Alexandre Henne's *Histoire du Règne de Charles-Quint en Belgique* (Brussels, 1858–60), ten volumes in three, in addition to the treatise by Nicolaus Vernulaeus on the origins and growth of the University of Louvain (Louvain, 1667).[78] One interesting donation, from The Right Honourable Earl Beauchamp, K. G., was *A Catalogue and Succession of the Kings* (London: William Jaggard, 1619). Compiled by 'Raphe Brooke Esquire, Yorke Herauld', the lineage of the kings and queens of Great Britain was presented from the Norman Conquest to the early seventeenth century. Evidently, the subject would have been of most import for students of British history. Nevertheless, at the bottom of the title page, a hand-written note in Latin indicated that the volume had been previously owned by the Franciscan friars of St Anthony of Padua in Louvain in 1760, and, it was therefore the Earl Beauchamp's intention to return it to Louvain.[79]

Even though the library that was destroyed in World War I was not the famous one from before the French confiscations, among the lost treasures – as emphasised by the international press – was a large collection of incunables. It is touching to see how several donors sought to replace these with special volumes from their own libraries. Among thirteen books given by Charles Thomas-Stanford of Preston Manor in Brighton, for example, two were early and valuable. The earliest was the 1496 edition of Cicero's *De Officiis cum Commentarius* (Venice: Pincius).[80] In this profoundly influential work of moral philosophy, Cicero modelled for his son how to lead an upright life in the public sphere. The folio printed by Filippo Pinzi also incorporated Cicero's *De Amicitia*, *De Senectute* and *Paradoxa*, together with early Renaissance commentaries. As was normal for humanist editions, Cicero's text appeared in blocks on the page, surrounded by the glosses.[81] Also donated by Thomas-Stanford was the first Greek printing of Pausanias's *Commentarii Graeciam Describentes*. In this unique ancient travelogue, Pausanias had described the monuments he saw and the religious and social customs he witnessed on a journey in southern Greece, in around AD 150. Among the notable features of the folio volume, issued by the Aldine Press in 1516, the ends of paragraphs were typeset to taper down on either side and form an attractive pattern on the page (Figure 4).

One of the most valuable donations, although it was not a Renaissance printing, was presented by the wealthy shipowner Percy Bates of Hinderton Hall in Cheshire.[82] It was a *Kelmscott Chaucer*, one of 425 copies on linen paper that

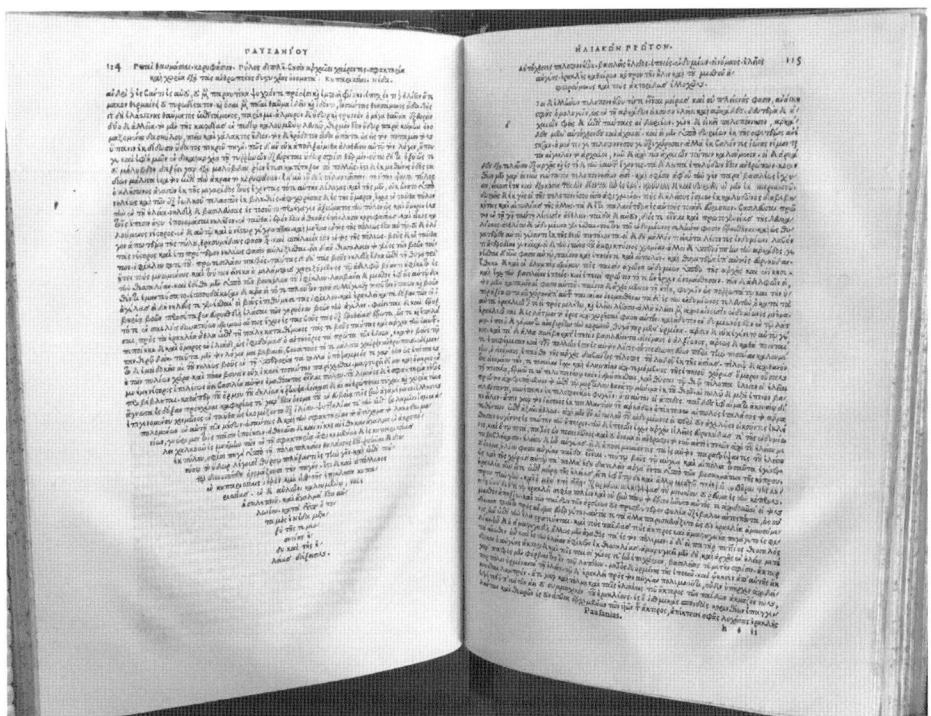

Figure 4 Pausanias, *Commentarii Graeciam Describentes*, in Greek (Venice: Aldus Manutius, 1516), opening at pages 114–15. Bodleian Libraries, University of Oxford, Byw. H. 2. 9.

had been printed by hand on the press established by William Morris and Emery Walker in Hammersmith, and published in the year of Morris's death, 1896. The illustrations were designed by Morris's close friend, the Pre-Raphaelite painter Edward Burne-Jones. Percy Bates corresponded with Guppy to ascertain whether the *Kelmscott Chaucer* had already been donated, and learning that it had not, wrote: 'I will send mine along as soon as I can get it properly packed, which is not an easy matter with so large a book.'[83] In October 2021, a *Kelmscott Chaucer* sold at auction in the United States for $68,750.[84]

Among the donors listed by Guppy in the *Bulletin*, several were academic institutions, scholarly societies, and libraries. In a similar manner to the John Rylands Library, these organisations donated from among their duplicates. Aberdeen University Library has already been mentioned, but some of the other institutional donors were: the Class of Logic, Queen Margaret College, University of Glasgow; the London School of Economics and Political Science; the Unitarian Home Missionary College, Manchester; the Clark University Library in Worcester, Massachusetts; the Classical Association; Durham University Library; the Master and Fellows of University College, Oxford; the Library of the House of Lords, London; and the Indian Museum in Calcutta. The institutional donations tended to be large, but in several instances the book titles were not recorded, since after August 1917, to reduce the space taken up in the journal, Guppy only published the name of the donor and size of the gift.

One example is the very generous donation by the Bodleian Library in Oxford, where the librarians during these years were Falconer Madan (1912–19) and Arthur Cowley (1919–31). As the Bodleian Archives reveal, the library's involvement in the Louvain initiative began in December 1915, when Falconer Madan was chosen as Oxford's delegate to sit on the committee set up by the British Academy to cooperate with the Institut de France in the collection of books for Louvain.[85] Thereafter, Madan was invited to attend committee meetings about once a month in London, and at the meeting of 15 December 1915, he recorded that: 'the John Rylands Library … [had taken] an early and prominent part in organizing a collection of books … already about 3000 in number'.[86] After Madan was made a member of the smaller Executive Committee, the chair, Lord Muir Mackenzie, invited Henry Guppy to London, on 18 December 1916, 'to tell us what he has done in the way of classifying and arranging the books which he has already collected for Louvain'.[87] Guppy was then placed on the Executive Committee to coordinate the work of securing 'offers of books and money' with Hugh Butler, librarian of the House of Lords and committee secretary.[88] Bodley's librarian, Madan, was also asked by Muir Mackenzie to communicate with 'college libraries and with bookish individuals' of Oxford to obtain donations, but few of the Oxford colleges had books to contribute.[89] Regarding the Bodleian Library's duplicates, the work of making an inventory was delayed because of the depleted staff complement during the war. The long list was completed on 15 March 1919, and forwarded to Manchester by Oxford's new librarian, Arthur Cowley. Guppy responded on 20 January 1920, stating that he would accept almost all of the books. Nine boxes and one parcel were sent to Manchester on 16 March 1920.[90]

Fortunately, the list of this extraordinary gift of 1,389 books survives in the Bodleian Archives. Since the books formed part of the central library of the University of Oxford, they were academic titles, mostly from the late nineteenth and early twentieth centuries. Numerous earlier works were also offered, though, including seven incunables, six of which Guppy accepted (since one had already been donated). Among these was a folio of Albertus Magnus, *De Animalibus*, from the Venetian press of Johannes and Gregorius de Gregoriis in 1495.[91] The respect Albertus garnered is reflected by the fact that this was one of five editions of the treatise to appear before 1500. Albertus offered interpretations of three works by Aristotle on animals, which were known from Arabic manuscripts, and also contributed his own empirical findings, as well as an encyclopedic dictionary of animals with entries that encompassed lore, scientific knowledge, and the practical uses of animals by humans. In a symbolic gesture of appreciation to the Bodleian Library and the University of Oxford for their comprehension of the tragedy and their generous gift of books, the University of Louvain sent an envelope holding pages from burned volumes, gathered from the ruins after the fire (Figure 5).

Figure 5 Envelope sent to Bodleian Library by University of Louvain with fragments of pages from burned volumes. Bodleian Libraries, University of Oxford, Library Records c.1542.

In a similar manner to the mention of the quantity of books from the Bodleian, there was only space in the *Bulletin* to record that the University of Toronto in Canada had given 1,229 volumes for Louvain. In the University of Toronto Archives, however, the exchange of letters between Guppy and the librarian, Hugh Hornby Langton, has been preserved, illuminating the details of their interaction and how a university on the other side of the Atlantic became involved. Spurred on by the published call from the British committee in London, the Library Committee in Toronto passed a resolution on 8 November 1916 to offer all available duplicates to the cause.[92] Separate from the donation to Louvain, Guppy and Langton had engaged in brief, polite correspondence on a regular basis for several years because the libraries exchanged copies of their publications. Guppy sent the *Bulletin* as each issue appeared in return for issues of the *University of Toronto Studies*. The bartering extended to include other publications by the John Rylands Library, particularly their facsimiles of notable manuscripts and incunables. To reciprocate, Langton sent volumes produced by humanities departments at his university, since Guppy had said that the sciences, medicine, engineering, and forestry, though strong fields in Toronto, were outside the sphere of the John Rylands Library.[93] From May 1919 onwards, however, the contribution of books for Louvain formed the main topic of their correspondence.

Initially, on 16 May, Langton wrote to Guppy because his letter announcing Toronto's desire to donate had not been answered by Hugh Butler in London. Then, as Langton explained, he had read in the *Westminster Gazette* that the coordination was actually in Guppy's hands, rather than Butler's. Langton, therefore, proposed to send Guppy a list of the library's duplicates, so that he could annotate it according to the needs of Louvain.[94] Guppy wrote on 3 June to apologise for the fact that Butler had not responded, on account of his poor health.[95] Assuring Langton that Toronto's duplicates would be welcome, Guppy also specified that the Rylands was acting as the deposit for the donations. Indeed, the library staff would soon start sending shipments to Belgium, since the university authorities were back in Louvain and were establishing a temporary library for the students.[96] On 8 July Langton sent the list of duplicates, and on 26 August Guppy returned it with his annotations. Guppy made a point of stressing the usefulness of Toronto's offerings because previous donations had not been strong in 'Science and Technology'.[97] Then, on 9 October, Langton wrote that he was arranging to have the books sent by freight as soon as possible, and that Toronto would take responsibility for the cost of shipping to Manchester. Langton also relayed how the Library Committee members had appreciated Guppy's enthusiasm and were 'delighted to think that so many of our duplicates will be of use'.[98] On 12 December, Guppy – as if to nudge Langton – reported that he had shipped 7,000 books to Louvain the previous week. Finally, in April 1920, Langton confirmed that eleven cases would soon be on their way.[99]

When Guppy announced the large donation from the University of Toronto in the *Bulletin*, he described the books as 'a valuable collection of general literature'.[100] In the University of Toronto Archives, only eight pages of what must have been a much longer list survive, and list the duplicates for Ancient Greece and Rome (on language, literature, and history) even though Guppy had selected mostly books on science and technology. Guppy's check marks show that about a hundred titles from these pages were chosen, including a recent study in German on the influence of Cicero through the ages, and the English translation of Apuleius's *The Apologia and Florida* (Oxford: Clarendon Press, 1909).[101]

It is evident from the number of books that Toronto was committed to the gift for Louvain. Two historical circumstances may help to explain this keen involvement. The first is that the University of Toronto had experienced the complete loss of its own library on 14 February 1890 as a result of an accidental fire that destroyed the eastern section of University College, where the library of some 30,000 books was housed.[102] Significantly, after the news of Toronto's loss had circulated, donations of books arrived to initiate a new library. Among the gifts from England, one that was given by the Bodleian Library has a bookplate on the flyleaf, which records: 'Toronto University Library. Presented by University of Oxford through the Committee formed in the Old Country to aid in replacing the loss caused by The disastrous Fire of February the 14th 1890'.[103] In other words, the University of Toronto had benefited greatly because a committee was created in England to donate books after the destruction of their library, and hence, Toronto responded in turn when another English committee was established to assist the Belgian university in their distress.

The second motivating factor was the presence of tens of thousands of Canadian soldiers in Belgium as part of the British Expeditionary Force. In a series of confrontations close to Ypres, including the tragic Battle of Passchendaele, the Germans used chemical warfare, and the list of Canadians dead and injured was terribly long. Students from the University of Toronto were sent to fight in Flanders Fields, and Langton and other members of the Library Committee would have known some who fell there. One expression of thanks by Belgium to Canada after the war was that a stone from the ruins of the University of Louvain Library was sent for inclusion in a war memorial known as the 'Garden of the Unforgotten', situated east of Toronto in Oshawa.[104]

At the John Rylands Library, in the years 1915–26, the receipt of over fifty thousand donated volumes and the preparation of the books for their journey to Louvain was time consuming. Guppy corresponded with many of the close to 700 donors and annotated their lists of contributions. Ultimately, 55,782 books were sent from Manchester.[105] Other staff at the library were preoccupied with essential repairs when books were submitted in poor condition: 632 books destined for Louvain, for instance, were sent to be bound in 1919–21.[106] To cover these expenses, Guppy had to solicit financial donations. Fortunately, the shipping of the crates of books was undertaken gratis by the Cork Steamship Company Ltd. The delivery began soon after the war had ended, and by the summer of 1920, four hundred cases holding about 30,500 volumes had arrived.[107] As students and faculty returned to Louvain, a temporary library holding close to 40,000 volumes, including those from Manchester, was arranged in the Institut Spoelberch. It was the intention of the Louvain authorities to keep what they described as the 'English Gift Library' separate, both on the shelves and in the catalogue, once Whitney Warren's new library had been constructed.[108] By setting the English donation apart, the Belgians recognised the special nature of the gift, which represented a vast library assembled from books that English and Commonwealth scholars, students and collectors had deemed important, although it was not, and could never have been, a direct replacement for the library that had been lost.

Guppy and other members of the British committee were also at pains to ensure that the English gift in no way serve to 'relieve Germany' from the obligations laid out in the Treaty of Versailles.[109] The peace treaty, signed to cease the hostilities at the end of World War I, specified the many reparations to which Germany had to comply. Among them, Article 247 required that Germany make restitution to Belgium for 'manuscripts, incunabula, printed books, maps and objects of collection corresponding in number and value to those destroyed in the burning by Germany of the Library of Louvain'.[110] The process involved calculating the value of what had been lost, which was estimated at 4 million German marks (in 1914), and then the purchase of books to reconstruct the original library holdings as best possible. This was not done by taking books from German libraries, but instead by purchasing from antiquarian booksellers, particularly at the international book fair in Leipzig, and buying en bloc the private libraries of academics who had died.[111]

In 1923, however, when Germany was struggling to fulfil the exacting obligations of the Treaty of Versailles, and Guppy was still coordinating the collection and shipping of the books for Louvain, another important university library was lost. In the immediate aftermath of the Great Japan Earthquake of 1 September 1923, one of the fires that was ignited destroyed the library of Tokyo Imperial University. In a manner that revealed his remarkable collegiality, Guppy expressed his willingness to coordinate a new book donation project for Tokyo.[112] The Bodleian Library also demonstrated generosity through the gift of sixty-six volumes that were selected by the Japanese university from a much longer list.[113]

But for Guppy, the recognition of the tragedy in Tokyo would have been fleeting in comparison to the despair that he felt when, during World War II, on the night of 16–17 May 1940, the University of Louvain's new library was shelled and most of the books, amounting to a collection of about 750,000 volumes, went up in flames. Two weeks after the second destruction, Guppy wrote a retrospective account of the collecting of close to 56,000 books for Louvain, which appeared in the British weekly, *The Spectator*. In this short article, some of the librarian's frustration was exposed by the strong language he chose when he characterised Louvain as 'twice-raped' and labelled the Germans as 'vandals' and 'invading hordes'.[114] Guppy also reflected on the collective meaning of the English gift library: donors had parted with 'treasured possessions' in memory of loved ones who had died in the war, and gifts of this nature 'partook of the sanctity of sacrifice'.[115] By meditating on the profound significance of the English gesture, Guppy evoked how tragic the loss was for those who were intimately involved. Indeed, as the obituary in *The Times* explained, Guppy experienced 'a severe blow' when the University of Louvain's new library – 'in some sense his child' – was destroyed.[116]

A few of the illuminated manuscripts and rare books in the University of Louvain Library had been moved to the safety of a bank vault, but, from a collection of over one million volumes, only about 15,000 survived.[117] Among the early printings that were part of the English gift library, the only one that I have been able to find still present in Leuven's Special Collections is Pausanias's *Commentarii Graeciam Describentes* (Venice: Aldine Press, 1516), with a bookplate attesting to the provenance from Charles Thomas-Stanford.[118] Some of the rare books from the English donation that were lost in 1940 were replaced soon afterwards when the library of Henri Omont, the late curator of manuscripts at the Bibliothèque Nationale in Paris, was purchased for Louvain. One example is the 1532 edition in Greek of Demosthenes's orations, which took the place of the volume donated by J. G. Milne in 1917.[119] It is interesting to discover that the two bibliophiles, Omont and Guppy, corresponded: in February 1921, Omont wrote after receiving Guppy's mailing of the recent *Bulletin* to stress the importance of a Latin manuscript from France in 1384, which was listed among those recently acquired by the John Rylands Library.[120] Little did they know that, twenty years later, after Omont had died and the University of Louvain's library was destroyed for a second time, early books from Omont's collection would fill some of the gaps that were left when the English donation coordinated by Guppy was lost.

Notes

1 C. Coppens (ed.), *Leuven in Books, Books in Leuven: The Oldest University of the Low Countries and Its Library* (Louvain: Louvain University Press, 1999), p. 133; E. Vanderweghe, 'Making History: The Destruction and (Re)construction of Old Belgian Towns During and After the First World War', in J. Mancini and K. Bresnahan (eds), *Architecture and Armed Conflict: The Politics of Destruction* (Abingdon: Routledge, 2015), pp. 182–97. For one assessment of the causes of the German attack on Louvain, see Wolfgang Schivelbusch, *Die Bibliothek von Löwen: Eine Episode aus der Zeit der Weltkriege* (Munich: Carl Hanser Verlag, 1988), pp. 15–17.

2 Schivelbusch, *Die Bibliothek von Löwen*, pp. 17–19; Coppens (ed.), *Leuven in Books*, pp. 104–9.

3 One was a sixteenth-century Dutch prayerbook: Coppens (ed.), *Leuven in Books*, pp. 136–8; C. Coppens, M. Derez and J. Roegiers (eds), *Leuven University Library 1425–2000* (Leuven: Leuven University Press, 2005), p. 165.

4 In issues of the *Bulletin of the John Rylands Library*, from April 1915 to August 1917, Henry Guppy discussed how the initiative arose to collect books for the 'devastated' library of the University of Louvain, beginning with a meeting of the governors of the John Rylands Library in December 1914, and developing by December 1916 into a cooperative project between the library and an official British government committee established by the President of the British Academy in London. See H. Guppy, 'Steps towards the Reconstruction of the Library of the University of Louvain', *Bulletin of the John Rylands Library*, 2 (1914–15), 145–54, at 145; H. Guppy, 'Library Notes and News' and 'Steps towards the Reconstruction of the Library of the University of

Louvain', *Bulletin of the John Rylands Library*, 2 (1914–15), 207–11 and 251–74, at 207 and 252; H. Guppy, 'Library Notes and News', and 'Steps towards the Reconstruction of the Library of the University of Louvain', *Bulletin of the John Rylands Library*, 3 (1916–17), 1–7 and 408–42, at 4 and 409; H. Guppy, 'Steps towards the Reconstruction of the Library of the University of Louvain', *Bulletin of the John Rylands Library*, 4 (1917–18), 124–78, at 126–7.

5 Coppens, Derez and Roegiers (eds), *Leuven University Library*, pp. 21–3.
6 Coppens (ed.), *Leuven in Books*, pp. 94–103.
7 L. Van der Essen, 'La Bibliothèque de l'Université de Louvain', *Bulletin of the John Rylands Library*, 2 (1914–15), 139–44, at 140.
8 On the fate of the library during the French wars on the continent, see Coppens, Derez and Roegiers (eds), *Leuven University Library*, pp. 37–50, 71–4.
9 Coppens, Derez and Roegiers (eds), *Leuven University Library*, pp. 37–50, 71–4.
10 Richard Ovenden, *Burning the Books: A History of the Deliberate Destruction of Knowledge* (Cambridge, MA: The Belknap Press of Harvard University Press, 2020), p. 109. On the size of the library in 1914, see Schivelbusch, *Die Bibliothek von Löwen*, pp. 19–24; Coppens, Derez and Roegiers (eds), *Leuven University Library*, pp. 101–8.
11 Van der Essen, 'La Bibliothèque de l'Université de Louvain', 141–3.
12 O. Steeno and M. Biesbrouck, 'Stolen and Lost Copies of Vesalius's Fabrica', *AMHA: Acta Medico-Historica Adriatica*, 10:2 (2012), 213–36, at 214–19.
13 The first book-length study of the library's destruction was by the German historian, W. Schivelbusch, *Die Bibliothek von Löwen* (1988). More recent examinations of the German retaliations in Belgium include J. Horne and A. Kramer, *German Atrocities, 1914: A History of Denial* (New Haven: Yale University Press, 2001), L. Zuckerman, *The Rape of Belgium: The Untold Story of World War I* (New York: New York University Press, 2004) and J. Lipkes, *Rehearsals: The German Army in Belgium* (Leuven: Leuven University Press, 2007).
14 Ovenden, *Burning the Books*; R. Knuth, *Libricide: The Regime-Sponsored Destruction of Books and Libraries in the Twentieth Century* (London: Praeger, 2003).
15 R. Bevan, in his influential book, *The Destruction of Memory: Architecture at War* (London: Reaktion Books, 2006), discusses Sarajevo's National Library (pp. 36–44), and the University of Louvain's Library (p. 205). See also V. Živković, 'Destruction of the University of Leuven Library in First World War and its Renovation in the Post-War Period', *Bosniaca*, 26 (2021), 112–22, at 121.
16 Examples include the exhibition at Museum Leuven in 2014 (with the publication J. Tollebeek and E. van Assche (eds), *Ravaged: Art and Culture in Times of Conflict* (Brussels: Mercatorfonds; New Haven and London: Yale University Press, 2014), and the conference at KU Leuven in 2015, with the publication, M. Collier (ed.), *What Do We Lose When We Lose a Library?* (Leuven: University Library, KU Leuven, 2016).
17 M. Derez, 'The Flames of Louvain: A Library as a Cultural Icon and a Political Vehicle', in Collier (ed.), *What Do We Lose When We Lose a Library?*, pp. 25–36.
18 J. van Impe, *The University Library of Leuven: Historical Walking Tour* (Leuven: Leuven University Press, 2006, 2nd edn, 2012), pp. 20–6.

19 Coppens, Derez and Roegiers (eds), *Leuven University Library*, pp. 172–9; C. Kott, '"Kultur"/ "Zivilisation"', in Tollebeek and Van Assche (eds), *Ravaged*, pp. 92–9; P. Buitenhuis, *The Great War of Words: British, American and Canadian Propaganda and Fiction, 1914–1933* (Vancouver: University of British Columbia Press; 1987), pp. 21–36.

20 The American donation of the new library building is discussed at length by Schivelbusch, *Die Bibliothek von Löwen*, pp. 123–68; and in Coppens, Derez and Roegiers (eds), *Leuven University Library*, pp. 191–275. For an American collegiate perspective, see 'America Will Finance Rebuilding of Library Destroyed by Fire in 1914: Movement to Replace Contents of Historic Structure Started Directly After Cessation of Hostilities', *The Harvard Crimson* (11 May 1922): www.thecrimson.com/article/1922/5/11/america-will-finance-rebuilding-of-library/ [accessed 22 March 2024].

21 T. Proctor, 'The Louvain Library and US Ambition in Interwar Belgium', *Journal of Contemporary History*, 50:2 (2015), 147–67, at 157.

22 For a political interpretation of the American involvement in Louvain, see S. Witt, 'Interwar Internationalism and the Rebuilding of the Catholic University of Louvain Library (1914–1928)', *Libraries: Culture, History, and Society*, 4:1 (2020), 1–28. On the inscription, see Coppens (ed.), *Leuven in Books*, pp. 173–4.

23 The Dutch committee, *Leuvensch Boekenfonds*, came together in late November 1914; see 'Bestuursvergadering van 21 November 1914', *Bijdragen tot de Taal-, Land- en Volkenkunde van Nederlandsch-Indië*, 70/3–4 (1915), pp. xii–xiv. The coordinating committee in Paris, *Oeuvre internationale pour la reconstitution de l'Université de Louvain*, was established in the final months of 1914, as recorded in *Bulletin de l'Oeuvre Internationale de Louvain*, 1919–28, and http://14-18.institut-de-france.fr/bibliotheque-universite-catholique louvain-succes.php [accessed 22 March 2024].

24 M. Derez, in Coppens, Derez and Roegiers (eds), *Leuven University Library*, pp. 131–9. Another extraordinary gift that has recently been commemorated was the donation of books by Japan after the end of the war; see J. Schmidt, W. Vande Walle and E. Mennens (eds), *Japanese Cultural Identity and Modernity in the 1920s: Japan's Book Donation to the University of Louvain* (Leuven: Leuven University Press, 2022).

25 H. Guppy, 'Twice-Raped Louvain', *The Spectator* (31 May 1940), 9; reprinted in the *Bulletin of the John Rylands Library*, 24:2 (1940), 250–54, at 252.

26 *Ibid*.

27 H. Guppy, 'The Re-birth of the Library of the University of Louvain', *Bulletin of the John Rylands Library*, 6 (1921–22), 531–44, at 537.

28 *Ibid*. For an American perspective on the celebrations, see F. Pierrepont Graves, 'The Story of the Library at Louvain', *The Scientific Monthly*, 28:2 (1929), 134–42.

29 The Rylands project is discussed by Witt, 'Interwar Internationalism', 15–17; Schivelbusch, *Die Bibliothek von Löwen*, pp. 117–18; Ovenden, *Burning the Books*, pp. 111–12; as well as by J. Hodgson, *John Rylands Library Blog*, 22 July 2014: https://rylandscollections.com/2014/07/22/centenary-of-the-destruction-of-the-university-of-leuven-library/ [accessed 22 March 2024]; 'Destruction of the University of Leuven Library', The University of Manchester: www.ww1.manchester.ac.uk/destruction-of-the-university-of-leuven-library/ [accessed 22 March 2024]; and C. Mills, 'For the

Love of Libraries: Leuven', *Hidden Europe*, 56 (Winter 2018–19), www.hiddeneurope.eu/for-the-love-of-libraries-leuven [accessed 22 March 2024].

30 See T. Koch, *The Leipzig Book Fair* (Evanston, Ill.: privately printed, 1923), p. 67. In Coppens, Derez and Roegiers (eds), *Leuven University Library*, p. 281, Guppy is named as the British coordinator, but the volumes are said to have totalled only 6,789.

31 Manchester, John Rylands Library (hereafter Manchester JRL), JRL/4/2/1/5.

32 In the John Rylands Library Council Minutebook, an entry from 1945 concerning the destruction of the University of Louvain's new library during World War II recorded the number of volumes from the English gift that had survived. Manchester JRL, JRL/1/3/2/6, p. 104; personal correspondence with E. Gow, University of Manchester Library, 22 December 2023.

33 *The Times* (29 August 1914), pp. 8–9.

34 H. Johnston, 'Other Protests', *The Times* (1 September 1914), p. 12.

35 F. Pollock, 'To the Editor of the Times', *The Times* (1 September 1914), p. 12.

36 *Convention (IV) respecting the Laws and Customs of War on Land and its annex: Regulations concerning the Laws and Customs of War on Land* (The Hague, 18 October 1907), Article 27; https://ihl-databases.icrc.org/en/ihl-treaties/hague-conv-iv-1907 [accessed 22 March 2024].

37 A. Evans, 'The Moral of the Holocaust. To the Editor of the Times', *The Times* (1 September 1914), p. 12.

38 *Ibid.*; The Versailles Treaty, 28 June 1919: https://avalon.law.yale.edu/subject_menus/versailles_menu.asp [accessed 22 March 2024].

39 'The Burning of Louvain', *The Times* (2 September 1914), p. 9. For caution about the comparison with Alexandria, see C. Higgins, 'The Destruction of the Library of Alexandria', in Collier (ed.), *What Do We Lose When We Lose a Library?*, pp. 69–75.

40 Guppy, 'Steps towards the Reconstruction', *Bulletin*, 2 (1914–15), 145.

41 H. Guppy, 'Library Notes and News', *Bulletin of the John Rylands Library*, 2 (1914–15), 99–113, at 107–8.

42 Guppy, 'Steps towards the Reconstruction', *Bulletin*, 4 (1917–18), 126–7.

43 See note 4, above.

44 Guppy, 'Library Notes and News', *Bulletin*, 2 (1914–15), 99–100.

45 Guppy, 'Steps towards the Reconstruction', *Bulletin*, 4 (1917–18), 126–7.

46 H. Guppy, 'The John Rylands Library: A Record of Twenty-One Years' Work. January 1900–January 1921', *Bulletin of the John Rylands Library*, 6 (1921–22), 11–68, at 11–14. For a comprehenisve analysis of Enriqueta Rylands and the foundation of the Rylands Library, see E. Gow, 'Enriqueta Rylands: The Public and Private Collecting of a Nonconformist Bibliophile, 1889–1908' (PhD dissertation, University of Manchester, 2023). See also E. Gow, *Enriqueta Rylands: Who Do You Think She Was? Discovering the Founder of the John Rylands Library* (Manchester: John Rylands University Library, 2008), and D. A. Farnie, 'Enriqueta Augustina Rylands, 1843–1908, Founder of the John Rylands Library', *Bulletin of the John Rylands Library*, 71 (1989), 3–38.

47 Guppy, 'The John Rylands Library', *Bulletin*, 6 (1921–22), 15. See also A. Lister, 'The Althorp Library of Second Earl Spencer, Now in the John Rylands University Library

of Manchester: Its Formation and Growth', *Bulletin of the John Rylands Library*, 71 (1989), 67–86.

48 F. Madan, 'Edward Gordon Duff (1863–1924)', *The Library*, ser. 4, vol. 5 (1925), 264-6; see also the website devoted to his papers at The Huntington Library, California: https://oac.cdlib.org/findaid/ark:/13030/tf8v19n9s0/entire_text/ [accessed 22 March 2024].

49 Guppy, 'The John Rylands Library', *Bulletin*, 6 (1921–22), 20; J. R. Hodgson, '"Spoils of Many a Distant Land": The Earls of Crawford and the Collecting of Oriental Manuscripts in the Nineteenth Century', *The Journal of Imperial and Commonwealth History*, 48 (2020), 1011–47; and N. Barker, *Bibliotheca Lindesiana: The Lives and Collections of Alexander William, 25th Earl of Crawford and 8th Earl of Balcarres and James Ludovic, 26th Earl of Crawford and 9th Earl of Balcarres* (London: Quaritch for the Roxburghe Club, 1978).

50 H. Guppy, 'Library Notes and News', *Bulletin of the John Rylands Library*, 2 (1914–15), 2–21, at 13; M. Tyson, 'Hand-List of the Collections of French and Italian manuscripts in the John Rylands Library', *Bulletin of the John Rylands Library*, 14:2 (1930), 563–628, at 597; K. Speight, 'The John Rylands Library Dante Collection', *Bulletin of the John Rylands Library*, 44:1 (1961), 175–212, at 176.

51 'Notes and News: Dr. Henry Guppy, C.B.E.', *Bulletin of the John Rylands Library*, 31 (1948), 173–9.

52 Guppy, 'Steps towards the Reconstruction', *Bulletin*, 2 (1914–15), 145.

53 *Ibid.*, 146. No copy of this register survives in the John Rylands Library, but a record in the John Rylands Library Council Minutebook for 1945 (see note 32) states that two volumes with the names of the donors to the English gift had survived the World War II destruction of the University of Louvain's library; personal correspondence with E. Gow, University of Manchester Library, 22 December 2023.

54 Van der Essen, 'La Bibliothèque de l'Université de Louvain', 139–44.

55 Guppy, 'Steps towards the Reconstruction', *Bulletin*, 2 (1914–15), 260.

56 *Ibid.*, 265–6.

57 *Ibid.*, 256.

58 *Ibid.*, 412–13.

59 H. Guppy, 'Steps towards the Reconstruction', *Bulletin*, 4 (1917–18), 125–78, at 163–4.

60 Guppy, 'Steps towards the Reconstruction', *Bulletin*, 2 (1914–15), 263 and 401.

61 *Ibid.*, 263, 271–2.

62 S. Fogelmark, *The Kallierges Pindar: A Study in Renaissance Greek Scholarship and Printing*, vol. 1 (Cologne: Verlag Jürgen Dinter, 2015), p. xiii.

63 *Ibid.*, p. 16.

64 I am grateful to the staff of the Thomas Fisher Rare Book Library at the University of Toronto, where I examined copies of the Pindar (D-10/00464), Demosthenes (E-10/00711), Van Adrichem (Regis F-00108), and *A Catalogue and Succession of the Kings* (Stc-00078).

65 D. Tangri, 'Demosthenes in the Renaissance: A Case Study on the Origins and Development of Scholarship on Athenian Oratory', *Viator*, 37 (2006), 545–82, at 545–6, 571.

66 Oporinus acknowledges Jacob Ruber as author of the commentary; see *ibid.*, 547.
67 For the printer's device of Hervagius, see https://marques.crai.ub.edu/en/printer/a11605170/a11605170_0 [accessed 22 March 2024].
68 Tangri, 'Demosthenes in the Renaissance', 561–3.
69 *Ibid.*, 572–5.
70 Guppy, 'Steps towards the Reconstruction', *Bulletin*, 4 (1917–18), 153.
71 Manchester JRL, JRL/4/1/1. I wish to thank the staff of the The University of Manchester Library for providing virtual visits to the archives when I could not travel there due to the British train strikes in spring 2023.
72 H. Guppy, 'Steps towards the Reconstruction', *Bulletin*, 3 (1916–17), 229–77, 408–42, at 237.
73 Christie's, *Beautiful Evidence: The Library of Edward Tufte* (2 December 2010): www.christies.com/en/lot/lot-5388542 [accessed 22 March 2024].
74 Guppy, 'Steps towards the Reconstruction', *Bulletin*, 3 (1916–17), 260.
75 For a coloured version of the Plan of Jerusalem, see https://en.wikipedia.org/wiki/Christian_van_Adrichem#/media/File:Jerusalem_map_van-Adrichem_1584.jpg [accessed 22 March 2024].
76 K. Nebenzahl, *Maps of the Holy Lands: Images of Terra Sancta through Two Millenia* (New York: Abbeville Press, 1986), p. 33.
77 Guppy, 'Steps towards the Reconstruction', *Bulletin*, 2 (1914–15), 272.
78 *Ibid.*, 262; Guppy, 'Steps towards the Reconstruction', *Bulletin*, 4 (1917–18), 136.
79 Guppy, 'Steps towards the Reconstruction', *Bulletin*, 2 (1914–15), 381.
80 *Ibid.*, 273.
81 A copy can be found in the Bodleian: Oxford, Bodleian Library, Auct. N. 2. 29. I wish to acknowledge the kind assistance of Oliver House and the Issue Desk staff of the Bodleian Library's Special Collections.
82 Guppy, 'Steps towards the Reconstruction', *Bulletin*, 2 (1914–15), 255.
83 Manchester JRL, JRL/4/1/1.
84 Christie's, *Fine Printed Books and Manuscripts Including Americana* (15 October 2021), https://onlineonly.christies.com/s/fine-printed-books-manuscripts-including-americana/kelmscott-chaucer-150/129857 [accessed 22 March 2024].
85 Oxford, Bodleian Library (hereafter Ox. Bod.), Library Records, *c.*1541, 'Donation of Duplicates to University of Louvain', 1920.
86 *Ibid.*
87 *Ibid.*
88 *Ibid.* Further documentation on the British Academy committee and the role played by Hugh Butler may survive either in the Parliamentary Archives or the House of Lords Library, London.
89 *Ibid.*
90 *Ibid.* See also H. Guppy, 'The Reconstruction of the Library of the University of Louvain', *Bulletin of the John Rylands Library*, 5:5 (1918–20), 504–14, at 510.
91 A copy can be found in the Bodleian: Ox. Bod. A I. II (2) Art. Seld, but in the Bodleian volume the treatise by Albertus is bound together with three works on animals by Aristotle.

92 H. H. Langton, 'Report of the Librarian', in *University of Toronto. President's Report. For the Year Ending 30th June, 1920*, pp. 19–20.
93 Toronto, University of Toronto Libraries (hereafter Toronto UTL), Archives, A68 001/054–060. I wish to thank the staff of the University of Toronto Archives for their assistance.
94 Toronto UTL, Archives, A68 001/062.
95 Less than three years later, Hugh Butler attempted suicide in a London hotel, and because he was from a prominent family, the incident was reported in the newspapers: 'A London Hotel Mystery – Mr. A. H. M. Butler Found Wounded', *The Times* (19 January 1922), p. 7; 'Mr. A. H. M. Butler – A Serious Throat Wound', *The Times* (20 January 1922), p. 7.
96 Toronto UTL, Archives, A68 001/060.
97 *Ibid.*
98 Toronto UTL, Archives, A68 001/061–64.
99 Toronto UTL, Archives, A68 001/065.
100 Guppy, 'The Reconstruction of the Library', *Bulletin*, 5:5 (1918–20), 506.
101 Toronto UTL, Archives, A68 001/061.
102 See https://exhibits.library.utoronto.ca/exhibits/show/utl125/item/3708 [accessed 22 March 2024]; www.blogto.com/city/2020/02/remembering-time-u-t-burned-down-valentines-day-more-100-years-ago/ [accessed 22 March 2024]; https://torontopubliclibrary.typepad.com/local-history-genealogy/2017/02/remembering-the-1890-fire-at-the-university-of-toronto-february-14-snapshots-in-history.html [accessed 22 March 2024].
103 F. Douce, *Catalogue of the Printed Books and Manuscripts bequeathed by Francis Douce, Esq. to the Bodleian Library* (Oxford: University Press, 1840).
104 See www.cdli.ca/monuments/on/oshawa.htm [accessed 22 March 2024].
105 H. Guppy, 'Library Notes and News', *Bulletin of the John Rylands Library*, 10 (1926), 1–21, at 9.
106 Manchester JRL, JRL/6/3/5/3.
107 Guppy, 'The Reconstruction of the Library', *Bulletin*, 5:5 (1918–20), 506, 510.
108 Guppy, 'The Re-birth', *Bulletin*, 6 (1921–22), 538–9.
109 *Ibid.*, 538.
110 See https://avalon.law.yale.edu/imt/partviii.asp [accessed 22 March 2024].
111 Koch, *The Leipzig Book Fair*, pp. 53–66; Coppens (ed.), *Leuven in Books*, pp. 152–3.
112 H. Guppy, 'Library Notes and News', *Bulletin of the John Rylands Library*, 8 (1924), 1–14, at 1–2.
113 Ox. Bod., Library Records, c.1543.
114 Guppy, 'Twice-Raped Louvain', 250, 253.
115 *Ibid.*, 254.
116 'Notes and News: Dr. Henry Guppy, C.B.E.', *Bulletin*, 31:2 (December 1948), 179.
117 Coppens, Derez and Roegiers (eds), *Leuven University Library*, p. 320; Coppens (ed.), *Leuven in Books*, p. 160.
118 KU Leuven Libraries Special Collections, BRES: Tabularium – Magazijn; RB1183.

119 KU Leuven Libraries Special Collections, BRES: Tabularium – Magazijn; R3B3937.
120 Manchester JRL, JRL/4/2/1/5; Omont was referring to MS 242 in R. Fawtier, 'Hand-List of Additions to the Collection of Latin Manuscripts in the John Rylands Library, 1908–1920', *Bulletin of the John Rylands Library*, 6 (1921–22), 186–206.